PRAISE FOR ~~ON MESSAGE~~

"The great film producer Richard Zanuck once said, 'The most important thing is the story . . . Not the script . . . but the story.' It's the story people remember, the reason they love a movie. Zach Friend, something of a genius, figured out that's not just true about our favorite movies. It's true about everything anyone wants to tell you—or sell you. 'Things go better with Coke' promises you not just a great-tasting drink but a great meal experience.' 'Tell me a story, Daddy'—What your kid is really saying is 'Help me go to sleep in a nice way.' Zanuck was right. So is Zach Friend."

—Chris Matthews, Host of MSNBC's *Hardball*

"Whether calling upon his own experience with the 2008 Barack Obama campaign or mining wonderful nuggets of dialogue from quirky movies like *Best in Show*, Zach Friend has written an entertaining and insightful guide to crafting messages in business, life, and politics. And as much as I personally chafe as a reporter over excessive message discipline in politics, I have to admit that in the real world his advice is dead-on."

—Walter Shapiro, political columnist, former Washington Bureau Chief for Salon.com

"Zach Friend is so good at creating successful messaging, he convinced me to read his book on messaging. He is THAT GOOD."

—Lizz Winstead, Co-creator of *The Daily Show with Jon Stewart*

"From a police department to the presidency, Zach Friend has been on the front lines of communications. Zach's book, *On Message,* has something to teach everyone, from experienced leaders to political newbies."

—Jamal Simmons, political professional and analyst

"*On Message* is exactly the kind of reminder that we can all use when telling our stories."

—Heather Stephenson, Co-founder and CEO of The Old School, former CEO of IdealBite.com

"Today, new streams of information are trained on us like so many fire hoses. In self-defense we filter most of it out. What gets through? It's not data, facts, or slogans. It's a good story. In *On Message*, Zach Friend shows us how great narrative evokes emotion, spurs engagement, and creates action. Best of all, Friend practices what he preaches: this book is loaded with stories from business, politics, and yes, even children's literature, to bring his concepts to life in ways we can all relate to and use."

—Gary Stockman, former CEO of global public relations firm Porter Novelli

"For giving a behind-the-scenes insight and the secrets of successful political campaigns, Zach nails it. He has written an illustrative and compelling book that is a must read for anyone who wants the real story. Business leaders, elected officials, and anyone who wants to be successful in message needs to read this book."

—Debbie Mesloh, political advisor and corporate executive, Director of Government and Public Affairs at Gap Inc.

"This book is a road map for success in creating powerful, lasting messages that will help you stand out in an information-overloaded world. Use it as a manual for developing winning communications that really connect with your audience."

—Donnie Fowler, political TV commentator, National Field Director for Al Gore for President, former Vice President of TechNet

"*On Message* has the kind of practical messaging approaches that newcomers and veterans alike can harness."

—Mike Maser, former SVP Marketing at AOL, current CEO of FitStar

Chippewa Valley Technical College
Library
620 W. Clairemont Ave.
Eau Claire, WI 54701

ON
MESSAGE

ON MESSAGE

HOW A COMPELLING NARRATIVE WILL MAKE YOUR
ORGANIZATION SUCCEED

ZACH FRIEND

TURNER
PUBLISHING COMPANY

Turner Publishing Company
200 4th Avenue North • Suite 950 Nashville, Tennessee 37219
445 Park Avenue • 9th Floor New York, NY 10022

www.turnerpublishing.com

On Message: How a Compelling Narrative Will Make Your Organization Succeed

Copyright © 2013 Zach Friend. All rights reserved. This book or any part thereof may
not be reproduced or transmitted in any form or by any means, electronic or mechanical,
including photocopying, recording, or by any information storage and retrieval system,
without permission in writing from the publisher.

Cover design: Gina Binkley
Book design: Kym Whitley

Library of Congress Catalog-in-Publishing Data

Friend, Zach.
 On message : how a compelling narrative will make your organization succeed / Zach
Friend.
    pages cm
   ISBN 978-1-62045-372-8 (pbk.)
1. Communication in management--Psychological aspects. 2. Storytelling--Psychological
aspects. 3. Branding (Marketing)--Psychological aspects. I. Title.
 HD30.3.F755 2013
 658.8'5--dc23

                              2013025153

Printed in the United States of America
13 14 15 16 17 18 0 9 8 7 6 5 4 3 2 1

For Tina

CONTENTS

ON
MESSAGE

INTRODUCTION

The kids in Room 207 were misbehaving again. Spitballs stuck to the ceiling. Paper planes whizzed through the air. They were the worst-behaved class in the whole school."

The teacher read these words from Harry Allard's iconic book *Miss Nelson Is Missing!* to my niece's kindergarten class that late summer day.

There are times in the summer in San Diego when you wonder why anyone pays attention to anything other than the outside world. Warm days, warm nights, and parents that tell you to get outside before you drive them crazy. This was one of those days.

I'd showed up to my niece's class a few minutes early and decided to stand in the back and watch. I had been visiting my family during a college break after a quarter in which I'd taken a dreaded astronomy class. Each class period the professor would drone out a daily roll call that reminded me of Ben Stein in *Ferris Bueller's Day Off*. It was bad enough that I was a humanities student taking this class only to fulfill an unmet science credit. But what did I ever do in life to deserve a class consisting of reams of overhead projections full of mathematical theorems and boring data? Whatever happened to the pictures of the supernovas?

In contrast, this kindergarten room was filled with pictures and colors; visuals that spoke more than words ever could. It was 85 degrees outside and the beach was calling, but in the room, even this late in the school day, the group of six-year-olds was captivated.

As the teacher read, she explained that Miss Nelson is a grade school teacher who never yelled and gave the easiest assignments. But her students took advantage of her, misbehaving and showing disrespect.

One day, Miss Nelson does not come to school. She is replaced by a substitute, Miss Viola Swamp, who is strict and loads the kids down with homework. The students become discouraged and hope that Miss Nelson comes back. Eventually, Miss Nelson returns to class and the children rejoice. Of course, Miss Swamp was Miss Nelson all along . . . just in a costume.

My niece's classmates were enthralled by the story. After all, this was a class just like their class with a teacher just like theirs. They were learning about the complex subjects of respect, teamwork, and responsibility. But they were doing it through a simple story.

It got me wondering.

How is it that a teacher can keep the attention of this group of kids, especially in a hot classroom at the end of the day? Why do college professors, like my astronomy teacher, unsuccessfully communicate with statistics and facts while kindergarten teachers captivate through stories?

The answer is simple.

Kindergarten teachers have discovered the secret to communications: in order to captivate an audience and engage them in the message you seek to communicate, you have to use the principle of storytelling—an emotional narrative.

The concept of an emotional narrative has been expressed for centuries by well-known historical figures. In twenty seconds John F. Kennedy challenged us to "ask not what your country can do for you" while Martin Luther King beautifully said, "I have a dream."

Why did these statements stick?

Also, why do you easily remember your child's birthday but can't remember the years of the First World War or the date you started your last job?

Again, it's simple. One set has a personal, emotional component and the others do not. Kennedy and King were able to build on emotional narratives with some of the most powerful twenty-second statements in our history. They didn't waste time with complex messages or fact-laden rhetoric.

They built an emotional narrative.

Have you ever wondered why terms like "death tax" resonate? Or how it is that everyone knows the logo for Target but not for US Airways?

Why do CEOs and politicians spend years thinking about what they are going to say when more than 90 percent of communication is how things are said? And just what does the 250-year-old Gresham's Law of Information tell us about how to use social media effectively?

On Message answers these questions through a common link: emotion and narratives.

A Simple Guide to This Book

This book features a collection of easy-to-read stories, and insights from politics, advertising, business, entertainment, and social psychology. It lays out a step-by-step plan of how to create a long-lasting winning narrative for your business, organization, or campaign through stories, emotion, and effective messaging. It's a simple how-to for building a powerful, emotional narrative; and why that narrative works.

Let's face it—theory can be boring. Otherwise, we'd have a lot more theorists in this world. Without relying heavily on complex concepts or data (i.e., theory), this book shows that there is an empirical basis for creating an emotional narrative, simple core message, and more.

Each chapter provides practical ways to build your own brand:

Chapters 1 and 2 focus on the building blocks: narrative and messaging. These chapters describe the development of an emotional narrative and message and reveal why people can communicate better with stories than with data. Through simple and familiar examples, each chapter will show how to create an effective emotional narrative and provide a how-to section on message development, including a message box and the power of the 2x2 matrix.

Did you know that more than 75 percent of communication is nonverbal? **Chapter 3** focuses on the power of nonverbal communication and explains how to be aware of what you are communicating without words. **Chapter 4** takes you into branding and helps answer why most people know the logo for Target, Nike, and Apple but not for US Airways. This chapter provides examples of successful—and unsuccessful—branding and how you can create a brand that will last for your business, nonprofit, or organization, or for yourself.

Chapter 5 focuses on images and helps explain why college professors unsuccessfully communicate with statistics and facts while kindergarten teachers captivate through stories and pictures. It attests to the success of using imagery in your business communication to persuade your audience to support your goals. Furthermore, it demonstrates the power of images and the relationship between pictures and memory. So often we believe that data provides the basis for proving facts and retaining information. But, as this chapter illustrates, cognitive psychologists have shown that images last much longer in memory than data alone.

Chapter 6 shows how effective communicators use emotionally compelling frames to help shape public opinion. It explains why terms like "death tax" work. Terms like this are frames, or ways of presenting the same information in different ways.

Chapter 7 will show you how to use small amounts of personal, emotional information to have the greatest social media impact. The chapter shows what the 250-year-old Gresham's Law of Information tells us about how to use social media effectively; it also explains how to generate traditional media coverage though social media and why credibility still matters—even in a digital world.

CHAPTER 1

NARRATIVE

How the Berenstain Bears Know Why Narrative Rules

When I was a kid my parents read to me from the Berenstain Bears collection of children's books.

In fact, I consumed them with such interest that it became a weekend tradition to hit the local garage sales in search of book replenishment. I demanded all Bears all the time. From pajamas to linens I wanted to see Papa and Mama Bear constantly smiling at me.

At the time I didn't know I was being sold their brand through an effective narrative. And quite frankly, my parents didn't care as long as I went to bed on time.

But what's telling is how the authors did it; they established a trusted narrative through something as simple as a children's story.

If you're not familiar with the Bears and their 300-plus books, you're missing out on a key element of narrative.

The Berenstain Bears' rhythmic authors, Stan and Jan Berenstain, told complex stories of job loss, friendship, trust, new babies, and more through simple and emotional stories. They established a bond with the reader; you trusted the family—after all they were like your family. You began to emotionally relate with the books as they told stories about moving or new siblings or even the difficulty of money in the household.

They told intricate stories in an accessible way.

Each book often had a story arc complete with a plot, conflict, and clear moral resolution to the issue. Over time the Berenstains established a narrative of a family, just like yours, that was working hard and doing everything they could to make the right decisions despite difficult circumstances.

It was easy to trust the Bears.

Their product brand was a direct offshoot of this narrative. They sold products that were kid-friendly and mother-approved.

I'm pretty sure there are no sanctioned Berenstain Bears lingerie.

Under this established narrative the authors were able to successfully sell more than 250 million copies of their books worldwide. And they were able to do it through storytelling.

Why is this possible?

Marco Iacoboni, a professor of biobehavioral sciences at UCLA, claims we are physically wired to learn through storytelling.

"Evolution shaped our brains to learn through narrative," he notes. In fact, he believes that our physiology allows us to emotionally engage with stories in ways we can't with data alone.

Jerome Bruner, one of the leaders of cognitive psychology, noted that children communicate through simple stories even before they can effectively speak.

We have evolved to establish narratives in order to organize complex thoughts. In other words, *nothing* is more important than the narrative.

We *want* to learn from stories.

We *want* to organize our lives in a narrative way.

We *want* to connect emotionally.

All other elements—framing, messaging, branding—need to be based on these narratives.

One way to look at it is that narrative is the foundation by which you build your brand. Just as buildings cannot be built without a strong foundation, neither can a business or a political campaign be built without a compelling narrative.

And the rewards of a successful narrative will become clear.

Thaler Pekar, a frequent lecturer at Columbia University and an expert on the power of storytelling claims that when an organization embraces narrative and applies it throughout its work, brand identity is clear and appealing; audiences are quickly and sustainably engaged; and knowledge is easily gathered and shared.

One such organization that uses this power of narrative is the Susan G. Komen for the Cure, a nonprofit organization that bases their organizational narrative on emotionally compelling stories from cancer survivors and caregivers.

The narrative created through Komen and their ubiquitous pink ribbons is one of unity.

Through their powerful narrative the organization has created a viral product that has engaged their target audiences and has shared a complex message of support through the wearing of a pink ribbon.

So how do you go about creating your own narrative?

Establishing Your Narrative

What exactly *is* a narrative?

In movies or literature narrative is simply the story. In politics and business it is your story.

For Toyota, it is an established story of reliability and quality. For Ronald Reagan, it is of optimism in America and conservative values. For the Salvation Army, it is the powerful impact your donation can make on someone's life.

All of these narratives are so commonly accepted we don't even realize that they needed to be created in the first place.

Narrative translates *knowing* into *telling.*

It provides the bridge from facts and figures into something that we are wired to understand. In other words, narrative helps us interpret the world. It guides us to highlight certain things and ignore others. Narrative provides the framework for understanding complex issues and making sense of the world around us.

For your business, nonprofit, or political campaign, *everything* needs to flow from your narrative. If your narrative is weak, it will be defined for you. And if your messaging, framing, and branding are incongruent with your narrative you will, simply, lose.

All good narratives need to be constructed. And luckily, they all follow similar models of construction.

Tell Me a Story

Human beings have a passion for plots. Our lives, in many ways, are stories. We have a beginning, middle, and end—a story arc complete with a few interesting plot twists in between.

It's natural then that we want to organize our understanding in a narrative way. As University of Connecticut English professor Patrick Colm Hogan has noted, stories are shared in every society, in every age, and in every social context. Stories, in many ways, provide the greatest ability for us to understand and learn.

Behind even the abstractions of science, the professor Walter Ong wrote, there lies narrative of the scientific observations.

Why?

So we can understand the abstract elements more easily. Science students write up experiments, they narrate what they did and what happened when they did it to provide the reader a clearer understanding of science.

Narratives help us learn. They help us take abstract concepts and understand them in our own constructs.

As British classicist Eric Havelock noted in his research, knowledge cannot be managed in elaborate, scientifically abstract categories. In fact, he points out that entire ancient cultures were focused on narrative and oral tradition, which influences how we learn and understand today.

Oral cultures cannot generate abstract categories so they "use stories of human action to store, organize and communicate much of what they know," Havelock says. Most oral cultures generate substantial narratives such as "stories of the Trojan wars among the ancient Greeks, the coyote stories among various Native American populations, and the spider stories in Belize," he continues.

Culturally we have evolved to understand complexity through

narratives. Oral traditions, which didn't have written text as a main communications method, used stories to teach.

Gustav Freytag, a German novelist and critic of the nineteenth century, observed that all effective stories follow a similar structure. Calling it Freytag's Pyramid, he constructed a pattern in the form of a pyramid to analyze the plot structure of dramas, which built upon a model that Aristotle had noted 2,000 years earlier. Freytag's observed method showed that narrative structure (introduction, conflict/struggle, resolution) was one of the most effective ways to communicate a story.

Now, more than 2,000 years later, kindergarten teachers, Hollywood producers and political speechwriters are still using the same narrative method.

What Makes a Good Narrative?

A good narrative is **simple, emotional,** and **true.**

It's unfortunate that the last part even needs to be pointed out but it seems that truth has become a prized commodity lately. And it's important to note that you can't create a false narrative and expect it will stand the test of time (right, Bernie Madoff?).

So how do you go about constructing a good narrative?

British literary critic Frank Kermode compared the structure of a narrative to the ticking of a clock: each *tick* creates an expectation for the corresponding *tock*. Specifically, the structure creates an expectation or challenge (tick) and a resolution (tock).

For example, think about a good movie you've seen recently in theaters. What made it good? It told a compelling emotional story. In fact, when a good story is told you ignore the fact that ninety minutes have passed sitting in a cramped theater.

Take one of my favorite movies, *Casablanca.*

Everybody loves *Casablanca,* or at least loves Humphrey Bogart and Ingrid Bergman. From the outset, the film creates serious tension and emotion. Here is the narrator's opening:

With the coming of the Second World War, many eyes in im-
prisoned Europe turned hopefully or desperately toward the
freedom of the Americas. Lisbon became the great embarka-
tion point. But not everybody could get to Lisbon directly. And
so a tortuous, roundabout refugee trail sprang up; Paris to Mar-
seilles, across the Mediterranean to Oran. Then by train—or
auto—or foot—across the rim of Africa to Casablanca in French
Morocco. Here—the fortunate ones through money, or influence,
or luck might obtain exit visas and scurry to Lisbon. And from
Lisbon to the new world. But the others wait in Casablanca. And
wait, and wait, and wait . . .

OK. So from the outset, you're "waiting" for the elements of the
good narrative to come out.

Well, the story strikes an emotional chord.

As MGM Studios described it, the movie is a story of "former lovers briefly united in the chaos of war. [. . .] Bogart is Rick, a world-
weary nightclub owner who claims, 'I stick my neck out for nobody.'
Bergman is Ilsa, fleeing the Nazis with her Resistance-hero husband.
Only Rick can help the pair escape, but he refuses . . . until Ilsa re-
awakens his idealism."

Emotion is high in this film. It ends (I don't think this is much of
a spoiler) at the peak of emotional resolution: Bogart risking it all so
his former lover can live a better life with her husband.

Why is it that we remember this film? Why do we remember lines
like "here's looking at you, kid" and "play it once, Sam, for old time's
sake?"

It is because Casablanca created an emotional narrative. A story
that resonated with the time and led the viewers through from beginning—challenge—to end—resolution.

These three elements are key.

As uber-successful movie producer and businessman Peter Guber
tells it, a good story has three main components:

➤ **Challenge**
➤ **Struggle**
➤ **Resolution**

Casablanca shows you the challenge of the difficulties in a war-torn area and the disincentive of sticking your neck out for anyone, to the struggle of Bogart meeting with his ex-lover just to see she is with her husband and needs his help in securing exit papers, to the ultimate resolution of Bogart doing everything possible to help his ex and her husband live a better life.

With this emotionally compelling narrative, the viewer was ready for the famous lines. But those lines would have meant nothing without the initial emotional connection.

Creating Your Own Narrative

So assuming you're not a writer for hit Hollywood films, how do you accomplish the three components of challenge, struggle, and resolution in your own narrative?

You can do it in three simple steps:

➤ First, you get your listeners' attention with a challenge or compelling question.

➤ Next, give your listeners an emotional experience by narrating the struggle to overcome that challenge or finding the answer to the opening question. In other words, allow each listener to put himself or herself at the center of the narrative.

➤ Finally, galvanize your listeners' response with a resolution that calls them to action.

Everyone from Hollywood and Wall Street executives down to mom-and-pop shops encouraging you to buy local uses this formula every single day.

Think about it.

Ever watch yogurt commercials?

The challenge: getting into that bathing suit for summer.

The struggle: overcoming chocolate cravings and your friend's peer pressure for pizza night.

The resolution? Hawaiian dream vacation with a perfectly fitting bathing suit.

Madison Avenue has this formula down. Notice that the commercial doesn't try and bog down the viewer with data.

When was the last time you saw a yogurt ad that said, "35 percent of our consumers will lose 3 pounds in 2 months while 25 percent will lose 5 pounds in 2 months?"

Never.

Data does not resonate in the same way the bathing suit does. But what's interesting is they are both saying *the same thing*.

After all, you may be only a few pounds shy of fitting into that suit. But the image of the suit resonates emotionally, not the boring data.

Why does this work?

A large part of the yogurt commercial's effectiveness is the ability to put the consumer in the center of the narrative. The customer watching the commercial easily empathizes with the plight of the person in the ad. They think, "Hey, that could be me!" And if the customer believes they can be the person in your story then they are more likely to connect. With the person in the ad.

The same thing rings true at the local level. Take, for example, your local bookstore.

The challenge: maintaining sales against Internet giants and big box stores.

The struggle: David fighting Goliath.

The resolution?

The consumer supporting their neighbors and buying local.

The bookstore ad doesn't focus on the percentage of lost sales or the tax advantage of Internet pricing or anything else that will lose your interest; the data are inherent in the image of David taking on Goliath.

And there is an emotional connection to your neighbors and locality that compels you to support them. You can see yourself fighting the big guy—you can easily put yourself at the center of the bookstore's narrative.

Often the challenge is depicted in terms of heroes and villains.

In the yogurt commercial the villain is your current body weight and the hero is your Key Lime Pie yogurt.

For local bookstores the Internet retailers are the villains and the hero is your friend and neighbor—the bookstore owner. In the world of cops and robbers . . . well that's self-explanatory.

In business, the hero is your product and the villain is the other product. In political campaigns the villain is simply the other candidate.

I know this does little to elevate the discourse in our society but there's a point.

The hero, as Peter Guber notes, "is the person, place, product or brand that enables your audience to *feel* the change your story promises." In other words, your hero will charge through to the call-to-action, the resolution.

Just like in every children's story and every made-for-TV movie, there is a hero. And in every political campaign the hero candidate is the savior to fix all of society's ills.

Let's look back at Susan G. Komen for the Cure again.

Remember, a compelling narrative should be **simple, emotional, and true.** It should offer up a challenge, put the audience at the center of the story (a struggle), and provide a resolution. We can deconstruct the Komen narrative to see if it meets all of these components.

Komen claims to be the "world's largest grassroots network of breast cancer survivors and activists fighting to save lives, empower people, ensure quality care for all, and energize science to find the cures. [We] are fighting every minute of every day to finish what we started and achieve our vision of a world without breast cancer."

Seems pretty straightforward. Especially on the hero and villain part (I'm pretty sure no one is rooting for cancer in this one).

Is the story they are trying to tell simple?

Yes: Komen wants to guide people through the breast cancer experience, save lives, and bring groups together (think the pink ribbon) to end breast cancer.

Is it emotional?

It's hard to imagine something more emotionally compelling than cancer survivors telling their stories and mobilizing groups to show strength, unity, and support.

Is it true?

Unfortunately, it is all too true. That is why the last part of their story is so important—to "energize science to find the cures." Breast cancer continues to be a major issue that needs advocates like Komen.

So, Komen met the first elements of a good narrative. But in order to ensure that the narrative resonates, they need to offer up a challenge, struggle, and resolution.

Does it?

CHALLENGE	AUDIENCE AT CENTER OF STORY	RESOLUTION
Komen presents two challenges within its narrative. Cancer is challenging enough. But second, it presents an empowerment component for those going through a cancer experience. Plus, it's easy to see that cancer is the villain in this story line.	The audience *is* the story in Komen organization. Through events including the Race for the Cure, other fund-raisers, and wearing pink ribbons, the audience is part of the struggle.	Working toward "our vision of a world without breast cancer." In other words, we are our own solution. Through unity, education, research, and more we can resolve this challenge.

Komen uses data to back up their stories but not to drive their stories. Their narrative is created through emotion and simplicity and resonates because of this.

When creating your own narrative you can use the simple matrix above to ensure that the following questions are answered: Is my narrative simple, emotional, and true? Does it provide a challenge, struggle (where the audience is the center of the story), and a resolution?

Coca-Cola Found a Hero in . . . Coca-Cola

The hero and villain method was extremely successful for Coca-Cola. Suffering from anemic sales in the 1980s, not to mention an identity crisis if you remember the various incarnations of Coke, former CEO Roberto Goizueta sought to jumpstart sales through targeting a villain: Pepsi. He used this method to rally his own employees and provide a clear vision for the company.

The result? Bringing back the original Coke formula.

Ultimately, the timeless flavor and unique formula of Coca-Cola was the narrative. It helped frame the choice between their product and Pepsi and eventually salvaged sales. The challenges for Coca-Cola were the sagging sales and the struggle against their villain: Pepsi. The resolution for Coca-Cola was not being Coke, but Coca-Cola. Being true to their original self. And they've worked hard to protect the narrative of originality ever since: They've gone back to being what they branded as "the real thing."

This isn't to say that when marketing yourself you should make yourself a hero. We'll leave that kind of ego to the late night motivational speakers. But you should put yourself in your narrative and then work to connect your story to those that you are looking to reach.

If you personalize it in a simple and emotional way, it will be easy for the audience to feel they can connect to your story.

Effective parents inherently get this. How often have you heard parents say, "I remember how I felt when that happened to me"? Such a comment places the parents at the center of the narrative, yet allows them to connect to their audience in a simple, emotional, and genuine way.

This American Life

I have a confession to make.

I listen to public radio.

When I'm not listening to how to get my car fixed on *Car Talk* or hoping to get Carl Kasell's voice on my home answering machine on *Wait Wait . . . Don't Tell Me!* I find myself checking out Ira Glass's master storytelling show, *This American Life.*

For those not familiar with *This American Life,* it is a weekly public radio show broadcast on more than 500 stations to about 1.8 million listeners.

The show is one of the most popular podcasts in the country and more than half a dozen of its stories have been made into movies.

Why?

The show translates *knowing* into *telling*. It takes complex issues, often from a first-person perspective, from prisons to poverty and even janitorial work at high schools, and turns them into engaging stories.

Ira Glass, the iconic host of the program, says that good narratives have typical building blocks or sequences.

They begin with a question that your story will answer and end with "a moment of reflection," a resolution that provides the answer to *why in the heck am I listening to this narrative?*

How do some of the most popular storytellers in the nation from *This American Life* create a compelling narrative?

By dedicating an entire show to Coca-Cola, of course.

Ever wonder just what is in the secret formula of Coca-Cola? So did *This American Life*.

We've all heard the rumors. The original version contained addictive stimulants; specifically cocaine. Of course, it was marketed originally as a medicinal product that could cure headaches and impotence. Not really sure that one would pass FDA muster.

But one thing we do know is the company has closely guarded the actual ingredients of Coca-Cola for more than a century.

Or have they?

This American Life found what appeared to be the recipe from an article in the *Atlanta Journal and Constitution* newspaper that ran on February 18, 1979.

That's right, the super-stealth trade secret ran in a major daily newspaper.

But was it true?

The show corroborated the formula with historian Mark Pendergrast who found a nearly identical formula in the Coca-Cola company archives.

"This was an amazing discovery," Ira Glass noted when he revealed the recipe on the weekly radio broadcast, "I got into this wondering if it might be possible that this super-secret recipe had been hiding in plain sight, in an old newspaper clipping, but once I learned it matched this recipe in Coke's own archives, written by the creator of Coke—it was hard not to get very excited."

After Glass read the ingredients on the air, the podcast of the show was so popular it crashed the show's website.

Why would tens of thousands of people flock to the show's website for the formula?

Coca-Cola has created such a powerful narrative of originality, and made the formula the focus of its brand and messaging, that bursting it seemed too good to be true. After all, people felt they finally had "the real thing."

Once the show aired, Coca-Cola was bombarded with media requests asking it to confirm the information that its secret formula had been cracked. A Coca-Cola spokeswoman told the *L.A. Times* that the show was close—but not quite there.

"Our formulation is our company's most valued trade secret, and we will not be coming forward with that formula," she said. She said that there is always media interest in Coca-Cola—"It's one of the world's most valuable trademarks."

She did confirm the legend of the formula to the *L.A. Times*—that it actually exists on paper, secure in a bank vault. As to rumors that only two people at the company know the formula at any given time? Well, that might be exaggerated. "We cannot confirm the number of people who are familiar with the formulation, but it is only a small handful," she said.

So the narrative lives on.

As for the most famous ingredient of Coca-Cola?

The first item listed in the recipe is "F.E. Coca," which stands for fluid extract of coca, which contains cocaine. *This American Life* claims cocaine was in the soda until 1903, and coca extract is still an ingredient in Coca-Cola. It's decocainized under federal supervision at a company called Stepan in New Jersey.

A cure for headaches and impotence? That might be for the next formulation.

But what's interesting here is how the show, through narrative, demonstrated the strength of Coca-Cola's narrative. Ira Glass followed his own model to create a successful narrative for *This American Life*.

So how did they do it?

The show started by presenting listeners with a question: Have you ever wondered what is actually in the super-secret Coca-Cola formula?

You know, *that* villain? The evil secret formula?

Here come the heroes. None other than a weekend public radio show. Not exactly superhero caliber but heroes nonetheless.

Next, the show took listeners through the journey, from finding the recipe in an old newspaper, to corroborating it through a historian, to even struggling to replicate the exact amounts in a lab with expert soda makers.

The audience could connect with this plot. After all, the radio heroes were struggling to crack the code that so many have wondered about . . . and they knew it wouldn't be easy (unless you consider the recipe showing up in a newspaper easy).

The resolution?

The show produced a drink that fooled one expert and was preferred by Brooklyn grocery store goers 6–4. Not exactly what math professors would consider statistically robust, but listeners were hooked.

This American Life's website was crashed and Coca-Cola was inundated with calls.

Not bad for a 25-minute narrative segment.

Even the MBA Kids Get It

Business *is* data. Think stock tables, balance sheets, financial statements, and things that actuaries get excited about.

But data is soooo boring.

Just ask the readers of Scott Adams's infinitely popular comic strip *Dilbert.*

As James Kouzes and Barry Posner showcase in their book, *Encouraging the Heart,* "Compared to the number of *Dilbert* cartoons, how many company memos and reports do you see posted in cubicles?" I've actually seen a few company memos hanging up in the accounting cubicles but the point is spot on.

Kouzes and Posner note that "numbers are abstractions from reality; the *story* is the reality." One of the reasons that *Dilbert* does so well is because he tells a story about balance sheets, business jargon, and personalities—in three short picture frames.

The comic works because it follows a process of narrative. The audience is able to put themselves at the center of his stories. Many of us are familiar with the challenges of work and we see the *Dilbert* scenarios as believable.

We are all part of the story.

And it turns out what works for *Dilbert* works in graduate school as well. More than thirty years ago Stanford University sociologists Joanne Martin and Melanie Powers did a study on using stories in organizations. They wanted to test whether MBA students, some of the most numbers-driven around, would respond best to stories or numbers.

As Kouzes and Posner highlight, the study compared the "persuasiveness of four methods of convincing the MBA students that a particular company truly practiced a policy of avoiding layoffs." The four methods were straightforward:

➤ First, they would tell a story to persuade people.
➤ Second, they would show data that seemed to prove the company had less involuntary turnover than its competitors.
➤ Third, they would combine data and a story.
➤ Last, they would use a policy statement from the executive of the company.

If you're like me, you're already bored thinking about reading a policy statement from the executive. So we can eliminate that one as the most effective.

So which of the other three methods worked the best?

According to the Stanford researchers, the story on its own.

In fact, the data-driven MBA students that were given just the story believed the claim about the policy the most *and* had the strongest recollection of the policy several months later.

Similar to the *Dilbert* cartoons, data alone couldn't convey what the story could.

Why Facts Alone Are Irrelevant

Luigi Pirandello, a Nobel Prize–winning novelist, laid it out in his Italian accent: "A fact is like a sack—it won't stand up if it's empty. To make it stand up, first you have to put in it all the reasons and feelings that caused it in the first place."

As Pirandello recognizes, facts alone do not convince people. Emotionally compelling narratives do.

This doesn't mean you get to be untruthful (nice try).

In fact, it means the opposite. It means you need to use narratives to present factual information. As Annette Simmons, lead author of *The Story Factor*, notes, a good story helps you influence the *interpretation* people give to facts. "Facts aren't influential until they *mean* something to someone," she states. Stories provide the context for the facts.

A team of researchers from Wharton School, Carnegie Mellon University, and the University of Oregon illustrated this "fact." The researchers were trying to figure out why people donate to charities. In other words, what motivates people to give?

As part of the study they designed a hypothetical fund-raising letter dealing with famine and poverty in Africa. The researchers designed a test using two different types of fund-raising letters—one that provided a significant amount of data and facts about famine in Africa, the number of children affected by food shortages, rainfall deficits in the region, and more. The other letter told an emotional story about a little girl in Mali named Rokia, and how any money donated would go to help support her and her family as they faced hardships.

Based on their results, the researchers showed that when people were given more facts and statistics about the problem a charity was trying to address, they were less likely to donate. The group that received the emotional narrative donated nearly 50 percent more than the group that received the fact-based letter. In fact, donors who were shown more details and facts about famine in Africa not only gave less but also were less likely to give at all.

The best approach for a charity raising money to feed hungry children in Mali, the team found, was to simply show potential donors a photograph of a starving child and tell a short narrative to them including her name and age. This provides an emotional context for the giver; and connected the facts of the situation (famine, children affected by food shortages) without explicitly needing to bog down that person with the data.

Annette Simmons puts it another way. When you want to influence people, say to donate to a charity, you need to get them to see more than their small piece of the picture. You need to break them out of tunnel vision.

Tunnel vision, she notes, is simply a form of denial, and facts bounce right off denial. Human beings see what they want to see and facts alone won't break through. "You need to be able to tell a story that stretches their awareness out of the tunnel and across the horizon. You must connect at an emotional level to draw someone out of his or her tunnel."

Now Go Do It

Tell your story.

One of the most powerful predictors to success in business, campaigns, and even nonprofit fund-raising campaigns is the strength of the narrative.

A narrative is your story. It should be simple, emotional, and true.

And nearly all great narratives follow a simple formula. They begin with a challenge, showcase the struggle, and end with a resolution.

How do you create your own narrative?

➤ First, get your listeners' attention with a challenge or question.

➤ Next, give your listeners an emotional experience by narrating the struggle to overcome that challenge or finding the answer to the opening question. In other words, allow each listener to put himself or herself at the center of the narrative.

➤ Finally, galvanize your listeners' response with a resolution that calls them to action.

CHALLENGE	AUDIENCE AT CENTER OF STORY	RESOLUTION
➤ What is the problem or challenge you are trying to solve? ➤ Is the challenge believable?	➤ Does the story put the audience at the center? ➤ Can the audience picture themselves in the struggle? ➤ Is the struggle believable?	➤ Does the narrative have a call to action? ➤ Does it offer up a resolution? ➤ Is your product, idea, or campaign part of the solution? ➤ Is the resolution believable?

Think back to Komen.

The **challenge** is breast cancer.

The **struggle** of the story is audience centric—the audience is the story in Komen.

The **resolution** is working toward "our vision of a world without breast cancer."

The challenge, struggle, and resolution are all believable, giving this organization the components of a powerful narrative.

When telling your story, focus on emotion over facts. Facts alone do not convince people, emotionally compelling narratives do. When building your narrative think about the emotional connection your audience will have to your story and think about what the facts you present mean to your audience. If you build this foundation, you will be able to set the stage for successfully communicating about your organization.

CHAPTER 2

MESSAGING

What will be your customer's takeaway?

All winning campaigns in the business, nonprofit, and political worlds have a common element: a powerful message. In fact, once you have established a narrative there is no greater factor driving success than a powerful message.

But what makes a winning message?

The answer is not obvious. First of all, it has little to do with information. And although it goes against conventional wisdom, money is not king in the land of messaging.

Which is good news.

You don't have to be a large corporation or a billionaire to "buy" a good message. You simply need to resonate; to connect in an emotionally compelling way.

But how do you do this?

Similar to constructing a quality narrative, a good message is, above all, a story—the story of how we're going to get from where we are to where we dream of being.

John F. Kennedy offered the New Frontier. Apple implored us to

Think Different. Even Southwest Airlines has connected with our traveling desires, telling us to "grab your bag, it's on!"

Many people think those are just catchy slogans. They aren't. They are powerful stories, convincingly linking a present problem to a future solution. And most important, these messages helped solidify successful narratives.

So how have John Kennedy, Apple Inc., and Southwest Airlines, all with completely different interests and backgrounds, created a successful message?

Interestingly, they've followed a simple formula. And one way to understand the formula is through the lens of successful corporate, nonprofit, and political campaigns.

The first step?

Understanding what a message actually is.

What Is a Message?

So what exactly is a message?

One of the best ways to understand messaging is to look at political campaigns.

Ron Faucheux, a political strategist who has worked on more than 100 campaigns for political and corporate clients, boils it down this way: "Your message is your public rationale for running; it's the most compelling reason voters should vote for you and not for the opposition. Simply put, it's what you communicate to the electorate that positions you and your candidacy relative to your opposition."

Think about it: If you have a business you are trying to obtain the same goals as a political candidate. The voters in their case are the customers in yours. You are trying to get them to purchase your product instead of your competition's product, so you need to communicate the most compelling reason that your product should be purchased or your nonprofit should be funded.

Your message is this rationale; it is why *you* should be chosen over *them*. A good message will flow naturally from the narrative that you have created.

Take Southwest Airlines for example. As other airlines have hemorrhaged cash over the last decade, they have continued to expand and make a lot of people rich. They established a narrative of a different airline, willing to challenge the old approach of the legacy carriers. Want a fun, safe, and no-frills (read *cheap*) airline without the hassle of the other guys? Southwest is for you.

What's their message? "Grab your bag: it's on!"

Their message perfectly harmonizes with the narrative that they have worked so hard to cultivate. Flight attendants are allowed to have fun on board and aren't restricted to classic uniforms. Bag fees? That's for other airlines.

By breaking down their message, it's easy to see how it acts as a rationale to chose their airline over others.

Want a contrast?

Grab your bag on another airline and pay a baggage fee. This simple message reconnects back to Southwest's overarching narrative of being a different airline.

Southwest provided a rationale of why you should chose them over their competitors. But how did they create it?

One of the simplest ways is through the message formula.

Developing the Message Formula

Now that you know what a message is it's important to know what elements a message should *contain*.

Strong messages contain contrasts—your strengths versus your opponent's weaknesses, emotional and empathetic components, and, when possible, elements that inoculate your brand.

That may seem overwhelming. But these components can come easily into play by following step one of the message formula:

> ➤ **Step One: Developing Your Message Box**
> ➤ **Step Two: Constructing the Message**
> ➤ **Step Three: Testing the Message—A Message Box to Answer All Questions**

Step One: Developing Your Message Box

What exactly is a message box?

One of the best depictions of a message box was provided by Ron Faucheux in his book *Running for Office.* He explains that the purpose of a message box is simply to break down your message into four parts: what you will say about yourself, what you will say about your opponent/competitor, what your opponent will say about himself/herself, and what your opponent/competitor will say about you.

Using this box will help narrow down the core message of your business or political campaign. It will help frame the choice between your product and your competitor's product.

When creating your message box, your message elements should be able to answer yes to the following questions:

➤ Will this message appeal to the groups necessary to sell my product or win my campaign?

➤ Does this message zero-in on both my strengths and my opponent's weaknesses?

➤ Does the message apply uniquely to my business or my candidate?

➤ Is the message big enough (and not generic)?

➤ Am I a credible messenger of the message?

➤ Does the message help in some way to inoculate me on points where I am subject to attack?

➤ Does my message offer an emotional connection to my audience or empathize with an issue it is facing?

Using this framework I've created a hypothetical message box for Southwest Airlines versus a Legacy Carrier.

SOUTHWEST ON SOUTHWEST	SOUTHWEST ON LEGACY CARRIER
Southwest Airlines takes a new approach to air travel. Our focus will be on low fares, fun, and ease of travel, without the restrictions. ➤ No baggage fees ➤ No change fees ➤ Just serving peanuts	The legacy airlines treat customers like a number, providing less service for higher costs. They refuse to change and restrict choice. ➤ High baggage fees ➤ Large change fees ➤ Blackout dates / restrictions
LEGACY CARRIER ON LEGACY CARRIER	**LEGACY CARRIER ON SOUTHWEST**
Our airline rewards customers for loyalty with first class upgrades and free flights. We fly to more locations and offer larger options. ➤ Multiclass cabin ➤ International flights ➤ Larger reward program	Southwest strips down plane travel to the bare bones offering nothing but peanuts in return. You have limited destination options and no first class seats. ➤ No meals served on board ➤ Domestic-only flights ➤ Single cabin airlines

You can already start to see the contrasts the message box affords between the two brands. Southwest wants to be a different airline.

How are they different? They have no baggage fees, change fees, or expensive fares.

What do Legacy Carriers offer? Higher fees, more restrictions, and traditional services (first class seats).

Using the message box, let's break down the elements of their message: Grab a bag, it's on! (Note that a message box like this could also apply to some of their previous successful messaging campaigns such as "Southwest Airlines: THE low fare airline." And, "A symbol of freedom.")

➤ **Will this message appeal to the groups necessary to sell my product or win my campaign?**

Southwest is capitalizing on polling data that shows that the two biggest gripes by travelers are added travel fees and rude customer service. This message reminds people that on Southwest, you can grab your bag for free and have fun with us (it's on!).

➤ **Does this message zero-in on both your strengths and your opponent's weaknesses?**

One of Southwest Airlines' biggest strengths is their no-frills approach. This message (as does THE low fare airline message) directly speaks to their strengths and contrasts those with the legacy carriers' weaknesses.

➤ **Does the message apply uniquely to your business?**

Since Southwest is the only airline offering these types of freebies, yes, it is unique to them.

➤ **Is the message big enough (and not generic?)**

This message might not be as large as THE low fare airline, but it does speak to a significant gripe of travelers. One could argue the message doesn't quite hit on this point.

➤ **Are you a credible messenger of the message?**

Southwest might be the only credible messenger on this point—so yes.

➤ **Does the message help in some way to inoculate you on points where you are subject to attack?**

Assuming legacy carriers will be attacking Southwest on their lack of flight options, service amenities, and loyalty perks, this message does not inoculate them against those attacks. But the lightheartedness of the message does diffuse some of the barbs.

➤ **Does it offer an emotional connection to your audience or empathize with an issue it is facing?**

At first glance, "Grab a bag, it's on!" doesn't seem to offer much in the way of emotion or empathy. But a deeper look shows it hits on both points. Remember when travel was fun? Before the days of 3.4 ounce containers and shoe removal? Travel has inherent *emotional* connections for people and Southwest's messaging is trying to bring back the fun in travel. Remember when you didn't have to pay $200 for bag fees? Struggling to make ends meet? Southwest's "Grab a bag" *empathizes* with that plight.

Notice that through the development of the message box the following became apparent:

➤ The contrasts between the two brands (Southwest and legacy)
➤ The strengths of their brand and what they should emphasize
➤ Where to protect their brand against other brand's attacks

The contrasts help establish Southwest's public rationale for being a business. The message plays perfectly into their narrative and shows why someone should choose their brand over their competitor's brand.

The message also highlights the strength of their brand and although it isn't perfect on inoculation against a legacy brand attack, it affords enough strengths and lightheartedness to stand strong.

Apple and their Think Different campaign is also a perfect candidate for the message box. Over the last decade Apple has built a strong following of loyalists—positing their brand as the brand of innovation and change.

Below is an example message box for Apple and their attempts to differentiate their product from the ubiquitous PC. When you read the message box below, try to think about how you would create a message for Apple. What contrasts would you show? How would you emotionally connect with your audience? How would you empathize with the concerns of the PC owner?

APPLE ON APPLE	APPLE ON PC
We think different. Our products are designed to enrich lives and make technology intuitive. We constantly innovate. ➤ We create fun, functional products that perform flawlessly. ➤ Our product experience is second to none. ➤ We constantly strive to innovate and improve—placing customer first.	PCs focus so much on standardization that they turn out cookie-cutter products. They are behind the times on innovation and make products vulnerable to viruses and hackers. ➤ PCs are nonintuitive, complex, and prone to breaking. ➤ PCs focus on volume rather than quality. ➤ They focus less on innovation than on profit.

PC ON PC	PC ON APPLE
We develop products that are cheaper and more accessible to the mass market. It is easy to customize our products or buy software that is compatible. ➤ Our prices are more accessible to the average consumer. ➤ Our ubiquitous products make us the standard in computing. ➤ Trainings and customer service are more easily available on our products.	Apple makes specialty products that cost more and are incompatible with many platforms. Their proprietary products make you beholden to their brand. ➤ Apple is too expensive and too proprietary. ➤ Their products give you unfamiliar programs and are not compatible. ➤ Very few people know how to use, fix, or work with Apple products.

Looking at their hypothetical message box, we can deconstruct the "Think Different" campaign to see if it contains some of the key elements of a strong message.

➤ **Will this message appeal to the groups necessary to sell your product?**

Apple is targeting two sets of people: those who want to be different from the PC mold—customers on the cutting edge who are maybe even chic—and those who are simply fed up with PC performance or options. This campaign reaches both of those groups.

➤ **Does this message zero-in on both your strengths and your opponent's weaknesses?**

The strongest element about their Think Different campaign is the contrast it draws with the PC world. This is a strong yes.

➤ Does the message apply uniquely to your business?

Apple has staked their brand existence on being the alternative to the PC. This not only makes them the sole credible messenger of this message but also allows Think Different to apply uniquely to their business.

➤ Does it offer an emotional connection to your audience or empathize with an issue it is facing?

Yes. Think Different speaks directly to users who perceive themselves as outside of the mold. Be it a college student, indie rock hipster, or cutting-edge small business owner, the Apple brand connects with those wanting to break from the standard.

What works in the corporate world also works in the political sphere. Political campaigns are the main purveyors of messaging structure and the message box is a common tool in presidential campaigns.

In 2008, the Obama Campaign adopted "change we can believe in" as their overarching message. They played on different themes (such as hope) but always came back to "change" as the main theme. In 2012, the Obama Campaign continued on this theme with the simple message "forward." The message was step two of "change"—moving the country forward from policies of the past.

The Romney Campaign had multiple messages from the primary campaign through the general election. Their message transitioned between patriotism (Believe in America) to reform (Real Change. Day One). Ultimately, their campaign settled on the economic-themed "getting America working again" as their key message.

With this in mind, let's construct a message box for the 2012 election.

OBAMA ON OBAMA	OBAMA ON ROMNEY
Barack Obama is a change agent that is moving the country forward. His policies are placing America on a road to recovery, breaking from policies of the past to revive the American dream and create middle class opportunity. ➤ Fights for middle class ➤ Bringing a new era of foreign relations ➤ Fights for social justice and equality	Mitt Romney is stuck in the past. He supports the failed policies that hurt our economy and have burdened the middle class. ➤ Champions policies that lost jobs, put the nation in debt, and hurt our economy ➤ Wants to return to the George W. Bush course in foreign relations ➤ Flip-flops on social issues including abortion and gay marriage

ROMNEY ON ROMNEY	ROMNEY ON OBAMA
Mitt Romney is ready to get our country working again. He is a businessman who gets results. He is a reformer who will clean up Washington to make it more efficient. His private sector experience is essential in these difficult economic times. ➤ His decades of private sector experience give him the experience necessary to get the economy back on track. ➤ He will put America's security first. ➤ He is a reformer that puts policy ahead of politics.	Barack Obama policies have failed to get America back working again. He supports a government takeover of healthcare, the economy and social policy. ➤ More than forty months of unemployment over 8 percent—failed economic policies ➤ His foreign policy approach is weak and has lessened America's standing in the world ➤ He is beholdened to special interests including unions

Looking at the above message box you can see that the Obama message answers many of the questions outlined above.

Does Obama's message uniquely apply to him and is he a credible messenger? Yes.

Is the message big enough and does it speak to the coalition needed to win? Yes.

Does it draw stark contrasts that play on his strengths, emphasize his opponent's weaknesses, and inoculate him from attack? Yes.

The Romney message structure was much harder to construct. More important, the messaging was not big enough or flexible enough for the complexities of the 2012 political climate. For example, the Romney Campaign's dogmatic focus on the economy failed to acknowledge economic growth occurring in key swing states and demographic and social shifts in other states that made the economy not necessarily the primary issue.

As the campaign wore on and the economy showing signs of rebound it became easier to see why you'd want to focus on moving "forward" versus reverting to policies of the past. For states where demographic shifts had altered the political landscape, a candidate's stance on social issues was also an important ballot box motivator that wasn't addressed by the economy-only themed message.

You can try this message box exercise on all other presidential campaigns. I guarantee it will be harder to fill in the losing candidate's box—especially the square where the candidate would fill out what he or she says about himself or herself. In the case of Romney, he focused so much on economy that he struggled to draw contrasts throughout his message box.

The same thing applies in the corporate world. Think about a defunct brand and compare it to a similar brand that survived. Or look at successful nonprofits. Why do the Red Cross and World Wildlife Fund survive while other nonprofits struggle? If you were to create a message box for these successful organizations against those that have not survived you will see that they are able to answer all of the key questions in the box.

The message box is an essential first step in the message development formula because it helps organize thoughts and build the components of a strong message.

The 2x2 Matrix

Believe it or not there are scientific reasons for constructing the message box, designed as a 2x2 matrix. Studies have shown that the 2x2 matrix is a perfect way to help organize your thoughts. In fact, it has been used by businesses for years as a way to improve organizational thinking.

It's so prominent that a bestselling book was written called *The Power of the 2x2 Matrix*. In it, author Alex Lowy explains that the 2x2 matrix allows complex situations to be modeled in relatively simple terms. Situations are modeled as a "set of dueling interests" where you don't simply look for a single correct solution but rather "understanding, perspective and insight."

Why is this relevant? Successful messages always generate inherent contrasts; they emphasize the *dueling interests*.

Southwest Airlines contrasted its fresh approach to fares and baggage fees to that of the legacy carriers. Barack Obama contrasted change versus more of the same—in many ways the *exact same message* as Southwest Airlines.

To develop this matrix, it is essential to understand your customer and gain perspective on your opponent. With these two components, you will instinctively have what's necessary to generate an effective message. That is, if you have a more holistic understanding of the mood of your customers and the moves of your opponent, you will be able to approach your own message more deftly.

Lowy notes this key element of the matrix: If your two quadrants are well defined and clear, the "options will be rich in explanatory or provocative power. If this is not the case, it is usually worth redefining one or both." In other words, if you can't fill out these quadrants in such as way that you can lay out a compelling case, it's time to start messaging again.

In the case of the legacy carriers, the Legacy Carrier on Legacy Carrier quadrant fails to find relevance with the mood of the customer. Customers were not speaking out for more first class seats or international flights. They were looking for a safe and inexpensive way to get from Point A to Point B.

What emotional connection does it draw? What effective *relevant* contrast does it create?

Their message failed to resonate because it missed the mood of their customer base.

This leads to one of the key reasons that messages fail: they address only one of the quadrants of the 2x2 matrix.

It isn't enough to simply understand your strengths or even your opponent's weaknesses. You need to understand your own weaknesses and your opponent's strengths to see what would generate the most effective contrast.

In the legacy carriers' case, they had a solid understanding of their own strengths: experience, options, tradition. That's great. But they didn't have a strong understanding of Southwest's strengths or their own weaknesses. Their messaging campaigns have done nothing to inoculate against their greatest weaknesses: inflexibility, fees, and poor service.

In fact, the more the legacy carriers tout their tried and true methods the more they help Southwest draw the contrast that Southwest wants: change versus more of the same.

Often, if you develop a message based on only one of the quadrants, you will develop a message that fails to resonate. The message may not work with your narrative or may just be a hollow slogan.

So if you've successfully addressed all of the quadrants in the 2x2 matrix, how do you know if you've built the right message?

Step Two: Constructing the Message

Once you have created a message box, and organized your thoughts with clear contrasts, emotion, and inoculation, you need to construct your core message.

Remember, messages aren't simply slogans. Apple's Think Different and JFK's New Frontier encapsulate widespread elements of their brands within short clauses. These concise messages have complemented their established narratives and act as their 24-hour spokesmen.

Core messages should be able to do this.

Marty Boyer, a strategic communications specialist and former newspaper reporter, has broken down the three key elements of message development that Southwest, JFK, Apple, and others have all figured out. She explains that core messages are:

Concise

If you've gone through the message box exercise and believe your core message should be a page long then you are thinking too much like a college professor and not enough like a kindergarten teacher. Your core message should be one sentence.

Active

I recently saw a bumper sticker that said, "Give me ambiguity or give me something else." Your message needs to be on point. No ambiguity. And unlike most government manuals, put your words in an active voice. How would Apple's message sound if it were "Thought Different?" Not quite the inspiration we were looking for.

Empathetic and Emotional

There may be no more important element to messaging than this. If you can evoke an emotional response in your target audience your message will resonate. Just like a narrative should help the listener believe he or she is at the center of the story, so too should your message. Apple isn't imploring others to Think Different, it is imploring *you* to Think Different. You develop an emotional context with their product or they are empathizing with your plight as a PC owner.

So you've developed a message box and have your message down from a page to a sentence. You are confident it resonates and are using nothing but active language.

Time for step three: the test.

Step Three: Testing the Message—A Message Box to Answer All Questions

It's time to move beyond the 2x2 matrix.

Once you have created a core message, how do you know if it's the right one?

Just as important, how do you apply it?

There is a message box for this as well.

This message box will allow you to test your core message in a live situation and it's extremely simple to use. If it is used correctly, and with a solid core message, you will be able to answer any question you are asked.

This box is commonly used in prep for media interviews or debates but is just as relevant for sales presentations, speeches, and product development. If you are a nonprofit, this is a great way to answer questions in grant applications or create financial solicitation letters.

This message box also provides supporting messages that strengthen your argument. It will also help you realize the difference between a core message and a supporting message. The core message should be able to stand on its own.

If you could say only one thing to the world, what would it be? If you were sitting next to someone on a plane or had twenty seconds to pitch your product what would that core message be?

As Carmine Gallo, a noted communications consultant and author, has pointed out, the core message should be "Twitter friendly." You need to ask yourself, "What is the single most important thing I want my listener to know about my [product, service, brand, idea]?" That would become your core message.

"Make sure your headline fits in a Twitter post—no more than 140 characters. If you cannot explain your product or idea in 140 characters or less, go back to the drawing board." You can then support the core message with key stories, benefits, data, and examples.

Creation of this second message box is the third, and final, step in effective message development. To construct it, place your core message in the middle of the box and supporting messages in the other quadrants.

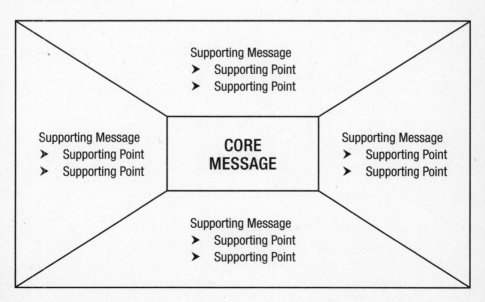

Let's take the 2012 campaign example and construct the message test. You will see how easy it is to organize the supporting messages and supporting points. Most important, you can see the difference between a core message and a supporting message as we test it with questions below.

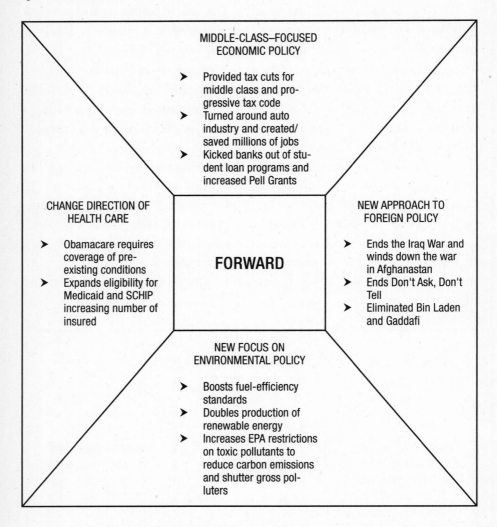

How do you apply this message box?

How do we know if "forward" should be the core message?

To test this, put yourself in the shoes of the campaign. Imagine you are being asked a question from a reporter:

"Madam Press Secretary, my understanding from Governor Romney's campaign is that here in Ohio manufacturing jobs have been lost and Governor Romney is saying President Obama doesn't have the private sector experience to address the issues. What do you say to that?"

Now taking the message box above, note how you can easily answer the question.

"What we need are policies that move us forward. President Obama has created a middle-class–focused economic policy for people here in Ohio, that turned around the auto industry, provded tax cuts for more than 98 percent of the residents and created jobs. And we know that when the economy is down people struggle to pay for things like health care. Which is why we have expanded Medicaid and access to children's health care so parents don't need to choose a mortgage payment over access to a pediatrician."

Core messages should stand alone. Moving the country "Forward," if that is the only thing that the press secretary could say, would be a strong answer to the question. The secondary messages support the core message.

The exact same thing applies in the nonprofit and corporate world. For nonprofits you can create this message box to test the core message on your grant application. You will be able to answer all of the questions within the grant application through this box, always pivoting back to your core message in your answers.

Let's take one more example from above and test the core message.

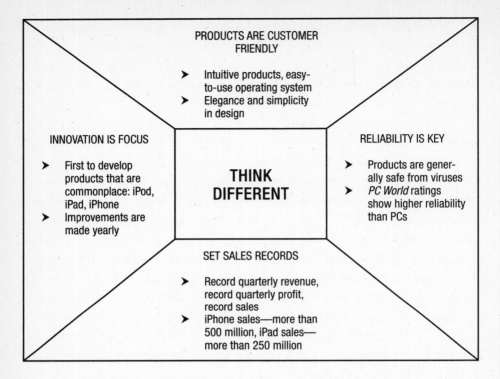

Using the Apple Think Different core message box, we can organize a boardroom investor presentation.

Similar to the campaign above, you can prep for questions from investors using this message box. Here would be an example intro:

"At Apple, we reject the belief that to succeed you must stagnate. That is why our customers and employees are encouraged to 'think different'—to expect more from their technology. Focusing on innovation and putting functionality and reliability first, we have set unparalleled sales and growth records."

Now take this method and apply it to a question from an investor. *"How can we believe that these sales numbers will continue to be sustainable?"*

"Apple doesn't fit standard company molds; we, and our consumers, 'think different.' That is why we have put iPhones in the hands of more than 500 million people and our iPad is owned by

more than 250 million people. The reason our sales will continue to grow is we focus on reliability, function, and design. Even PC World Magazine rated our products as more reliable than PCs. With support like that and an attitude to think different, we're confident these sales will continue."

With this second message box it becomes easy to test the strength of your core message. Apple, for example, wouldn't have been able to make their core message simply one of reliability.

While it is an important point, reliability shouldn't be the core or *only* point Apple gets across in that twenty-second pitch.

If Apple marketers were to sit next to you on the plane you would expect to hear them emphasize how their company, and their customers, are different. That is why they succeed.

With these tools—developing a message box, constructing a message, and testing a message—you've been able to create and test your core message. But what if you're still stuck? Here is a cheat sheet on common messages that work.

Messages that Work

There is no single catch-all message that will work every time. But there are some messages that seem to constantly find success. In fact, you can see some of these themes repeated throughout the examples above.

What is the most common message that resonates?

Change.

Not all change is good change. When my car's air conditioning system recently broke down the "change" cost me about $500.

Effective communicators frame change with a sense of hope and optimism.

Remember that a good message is, above all, a story—the story of how we're going to get from where we are to where we dream of being.

Political campaigns nearly always emphasize change (unless of course it is a candidate running for reelection!).

Southwest wants a change from the old ways of the airline industry. Apple Inc. wants you to change from the dominance of the PC world; to Think Different. In both cases their messaging gives you optimism that things *can* change and that change would be a good thing.

While change is the most fundamental message, there are others that resonate. A second common message is:

Pride and Determination.

Who doesn't want to have pride in what they're doing or pride in themselves?

Many companies have figured this out (especially in the athletic world) but so too has the government.

Two of the most successful usages of the pride and determination message scheme are from the United States Army, "An Army of One" and Nike, "Just do it."

Why do these work? They evoke an emotion. Pride is an emotion, and connecting with someone's desire to "just do it" is very powerful.

One last cheat sheet message that works?

Well, since you need to have emotion in your message you could always make emotion the message.

Emotion

In World War II the government was looking for an emotionally compelling message to help make the war effort relevant for the average citizen.

Its message? "Loose lips sink ships."

Imagine the emotional response this invokes. No one wants to be responsible for harming one of our own. So this messaging effectively connects using emotion.

Another example?

For those of you who own a diamond or had to pay a lot of money for one for someone you love, you can thank De Beers: "A Diamond is Forever." Everyone hopes his or her relationship will last forever (all right, not everyone). But there is an emotional response to the permanence of relationships. De Beers has effectively connected with this emotion and built its entire brand on this basis.

Change, Pride and Emotion.

By no means is this a comprehensive list of messages that work, but if you're stuck, these three are good starting points.

Now Go Do It

Creating an effective message might seem overwhelming but it becomes simple if you follow the three-step formula. To recap, here are the steps to successful message development:

➤ **Create a message box:** focus on your strengths and show contrasts with your competitor.
➤ **Develop your core message:** your message should evoke an emotion and clearly differentiate you from your competition. Make sure it is concise and active. A Twitter-friendly headline. No novel-length messages!
➤ **Test your message:** using the core message box you can see if your message stands the twenty-second test. Your core message should be able to stand alone—the one thing you would tell someone about your product or campaign if you had a chance.

Ask yourself the following questions:

➤ Will this message appeal to the groups necessary to sell my product or win my campaign?
➤ Does this message zero-in on both my strengths and my opponent's weaknesses?
➤ Does the message apply uniquely to my business or my candidate?
➤ Is the message big enough (and not generic?)
➤ Am I a credible messenger of the message?

➤ Does the message help in some way to inoculate me on points where I am subject to attack?

➤ Does it offer an emotional connection to my audience or empathize with an issue it is facing?

If you can answer "yes" to the questions above you are on pace to create a strong core message. The core message should be supported by two or three key stories, statistics, and examples that reinforce it.

All winning campaigns in the business, nonprofit, and political worlds have a powerful message. With this simple formula, you can easily create your own winning message that will help build your brand.

CHAPTER 3

NONVERBAL
COMMUNICATION

The Middle Finger Theory

Have you ever been cut off on a freeway by someone going 85 M.P.H.? Did you ever provide some emotional, nonverbal communication of your own? Perhaps . . . the middle finger?

Did it express as much, if not more, than the words you were thinking?

Looks like you've experienced the power of nonverbal communication.

Every day we communicate more without words than we do with words. In fact, it is the nonverbal context that helps us break through the complexity of language. It's the reason for those cheesy emoticons in e-mails—without nonverbal context, we draw all kinds of conclusions about what the e-mail *really* means.

Parents are masters of understanding nonverbal cues. If you have kids you know when they are lying to you. It's not that they've said, "Parents, listen up. I was lying to you when I said I ate my broccoli." So you had no *verbal* communication to know they were lying. But they sent nonverbal cues: feet shuffling, eyes not meeting your eyes, that *told* you they were lying.

If there was one thing my mother was good at it was nonverbal communication. When my two brothers or I messed up—a relatively common occurrence if you can imagine three boys growing up together—my mother had a way of giving a look, providing some silence, and raising a finger that showed we were about to receive the wrath.

But the wrath never came.

Because the nonverbal cues *were* the wrath.

Marjorie Fink Vargas, author of a seminal book on nonverbal communication entitled *Louder than Words,* shows some scientific data that helps provide the answer to why my mother was so effective.

Dozens of nonverbal systems are used to communicate between human beings, she notes, but nine of them contribute the most. My mother had three (actually maybe nine) down pat: Silence, eye contact, and kinesics (body movement and position). The other six are proximity, chronemics (time in its physiological dimension), color, touch, voice qualities that accompany the spoken word, and physical characteristics (age, physique, etc.).

Social scientists have shown that many nonverbal communication tools are learned and vary from culture to culture. Hand gestures in one country may communicate openness while in another might offend.

But the key theoretical finding is that nonverbal communication tools can be managed and taught. When you are communicating with your audience you need to think of the totality of how you are presenting.

Are your words congruent with your actions?

Are you connecting at a nonverbal level, with eye contact and gestures, in the same way you are verbally?

The influence of nonverbal connection especially holds true with CEOs, salespeople, and politicians. It's not just *what* they said that mattered. It's how you *felt* when they said it, based on the way they nonverbally communicated. The context of their words, or the way the words were delivered, communicated even more than what was actually said.

I know what you're thinking: "Wait a minute! Didn't we just spent a lot of time developing a narrative and a message and now you are you telling me those things don't matter?" Not exactly; I guarantee you won't succeed if you have a failed narrative and weak message.

But even with those things, it's important to understand how much you are saying even when you aren't actually speaking.

Most people think that nearly all communication is verbal, that the specific *types* of words you say are what matters. In fact, we spend more time focusing on *what* we are going to say without regard to *how* it will be received. Or even *how* we will deliver it.

Not quite.

Then what percentage of communication do you think is verbal?

That's a good question. To keep you in suspense I'll get to the exact percentages in a second.

First it's marriage story time.

Some Married Guys Fail to Communicate

Married guys need help in a lot of things.

But one thing they really need help at is understanding how words are interpreted—the power of nonverbal communication.

I have a friend that perfectly illustrates this. He's a former executive of a middle-sized company. We'll call him Married Guy X.

Mr. X met me in my office to seek my advice after getting into a disagreement with his wife. Mr. X told me that he was reading the paper when his wife asked if he was interested in going to a movie with her.

Naturally, he asked her what kind of movie it was. She responded by saying, "If you didn't want to go to a movie with me why didn't you say so?"

"What?" he had said. "I didn't say I wasn't interested in going to a movie."

Well, if you're reading this and are a married female you darn well know what Mr. X said. After all, he *said,* "There is no way I am going to spend this perfectly good Sunday afternoon watching some *Sleepless in Seattle* remake when football is on."

Sound familiar?

See, it's not what he said that mattered, it's how it made her feel. It was the contextual clues and nonverbal cues that gave him away. He told her all he needed to with his lack of nonverbal communication skills.

Dr. Daniel Goleman wrote a seminal book on emotional intelligence that can help show why Mr. X failed. Loosely defined, emotional intelligence factors in emotion as part of a person's intelligence; it is stepping beyond simple IQ to show the relationship between knowing and managing your own emotions and recognizing emotions in others to communicate better and succeed. It helps explain why we all have friends who are brilliant from an IQ standpoint but are unsuccessful by most of life's other measurements.

According to Dr. Goleman, people rarely put their emotions into words. "The key to intuiting another's feelings is in the ability to read nonverbal channels: tone of voice, gesture, facial expressions, and the like."

But Mr. X failed to pick up on this. Mr. X didn't even look up from his paper when his wife asked him about the movie.

Strike one.

While I wasn't there I'm pretty sure her tone would have sent him a clue that she was interested in the *Sleepless in Seattle* remake.

Strike two.

And while he didn't see her initial gesture upon asking he did see the exasperated gesture after his response.

Strike three.

This isn't exactly a *Men Are from Mars* moment, but it does show that while the mode for the rational mind is words, the mode of the emotions is nonverbal.

As Dr. Goleman notes, "When a person's words disagree with what is conveyed via his tone of voice, gesture or other nonverbal channel, the emotional truth is in *how* he says something rather than in *what* he says."

Apparently Mr. X *said*, "I plan on watching football" with his nonverbal cues.

Just what percentage of communication *is* verbal communication? Noted psychologist Anton Barbour has the answer . . . 7 percent.

That's right, only 7 percent.

According to Barbour, 38 percent of communication is vocal (volume, pitch, rhythm) while another 55 percent is body movement, such as facial expressions, eye movement, and hand movements.

That makes a cool 93 percent of communication nonverbal.

Some have argued that this verbal-nonverbal ratio is a bit of an overstatement but it still illustrates a key point: that we need to think of the totality of *how* we are communicating, not just *what* we are communicating.

Great communicators understand this. When was the last time you saw Ronald Reagan or Berkshire Hathaway CEO Warren Buffett give a speech where he had his back to the crowd or used the wrong tone?

In contrast, when was the last time you were inspired by a math teacher's monotone delivery? Ben Stein's "Bueller? . . . Bueller?" Anyone?

These nonverbal cues define you to your audience. Ben Stein came off as the boring economics teacher and it didn't really matter how brilliant his lecture on the Pythagorean theorem was. Why?

Because it was boring.

Great communicators understand that the context and tone of their delivery have significant impact on how their message is received.

Context? What Context?

How would you react if a political candidate spoke at a university rally and slumped over the microphone, shoulders down, soft voice, head turning side-to-side while saying, "Um, hello Madison. Are we going to win in November? You betcha."

What if the same candidate had taken the same soft-spoken approach, slumped over but yelled, "HELLO Madison!!! ARE WE GOING TO WIN IN NOVEMBER?!!" Aside from thinking the guy was crazy you'd realize this guy had swung and missed on context.

Watching this event on TV you'd think you were watching Improv Theater. This guy can't be serious, right?

What great corporate and political communicators understand is context. They understand that they can't go in front of a college crowd without energy. And they can't go in front of any crowd without sincerity. In this candidate's case the nonverbal cues would have screamed insincerity.

Your audience will develop expectations of what you will say and how you will say it based on the context of the situation. In the case of the college political speech, the audience would have expected it to be similar to a rally—and the candidate's speech and tone and nonverbal cues should have reflected its expectations.

It turns out there are smart people who have studied exactly this.

Neuroscientist Spencer D. Kelly co-authored a paper on how the brain interprets, and correlates, gestures and words. Specifically, one component of the paper described what happens when a person sees gestures that contradict the words that are being spoken.

Using a machine that measures brain waves in the form of peaks and valleys, the scientists showed that the brain reacts to this incongruence of words and gestures in the same way it would react to hearing nonsensical language.

So when you're speaking to a college crowd in Madison, slouched over, monotone yet projecting your voice like you're crazy, well . . . you come off as crazy.

And science proves it.

Your gestures and tones need to match your words. Your nonverbal cues need to harmonize with your words.

When done right, however, this harmony of words and nonverbal cues can have a powerful impact. In the context of a tragic event, your audience expects calm reassurance and a sense of control of the situation. Your body language and tone can dramatically defuse a tense situation.

One of the best examples of this contextual delivery came after the horrific events of September 11th, when Mayor Rudy Giuliani forged a lasting image in many people's minds. The United States had been attacked and there was a general sense of collective grieving. Things felt chaotic and out of place. Given the context, the country needed to hear—and see—that there was a sense of control over what felt uncontrollable. Mayor Giuliani ended up giving a short speech that reassured a grieving nation.

As the *New York Times* reported Mayor Giuliani's words:

> *"Today is obviously one of the most difficult days in the history of the city," he said softly. "The tragedy that we are undergoing right now is something that we've had nightmares about. My heart goes out to all the innocent victims of this horrible and vicious act of terrorism. And our focus now has to be to save as many lives as possible."*
>
> *The mayor looked up through his glasses, aware that among the viewers of this live broadcast were the mothers, fathers, spouses, lovers and children of those who labored in the smashed towers.*
>
> *"The number of casualties," he said, "will be more than any of us can bear ultimately."*

As *Success Magazine* noted, many experts have described the mayor's leadership style following the attacks as textbook. He spoke with a calm, trusted voice that reassured the country by detailing its steps to safety. He shared in the city's grief and consoled survivors while championing rescuers, everyday heroes, and the residents of New York City.

The mayor verbally presented an emotionally compelling story. But it is what he communicated without words, through the softness of his voice, the resolve in his tone, and his strength in presence that truly made an impact. These images were replayed on television and communicated universally.

How Often Do We Communicate Nonverbally?

It turns out we spend nearly all of our time communicating nonverbally.

Ray Birdwhistell, a noted anthropologist who studied nonverbal behavior, made some remarkable discoveries of the amount of nonverbal communication that takes place. Based on his research, he estimates "that the average person actually speaks words for a total of only 10–11 minutes daily" with the standard sentence "taking only about 2.5 seconds."

Therefore, Birdwhistell notes, the overwhelming amount of communication occurs *without words*.

Similar to the political candidate in Madison and to Mayor Giuliani in New York, you are communicating more without words than you are with words. I know what you're thinking. You wish you were this lucky. After all, most of your co-workers seem to talk for at least ten minutes just to figure out where to go to lunch. You *wish* they were communicating more nonverbally in that scenario.

But they are the outliers. And we'll leave studies of outliers to great books by Malcolm Gladwell.

So this overwhelming amount of nonverbal communication begs the obvious question: If you're communicating with words for only ten minutes per day how do you communicate effectively? If the average sentence is only 2.5 seconds long—how do you make sure you get your point across?

To reach your audience you need to understand that effective communication is the *combined* harmony of verbal and nonverbal actions. In other words, you need to think as much about what you're saying as *how* you are conveying what you're saying.

For example, you need the nonverbal cues to convey a sense of strength, when necessary, or vulnerability, when necessary. Thinking about Mayor Giuliani's speech, he blended a sense of strength and vulnerability based on words and tone.

You need your words to complement your body language. You need, especially if you're Mr. Married Guy X, to communicate with the totality of your body. Understanding this interrelationship can significantly help what you *intend* to say to be what you actually *convey*.

Put simply, nonverbal communication and verbal communication are connected.

Some social scientists have argued that nonverbal communication is necessary to support verbal communication. In other words, your gestures and voice and facial expressions provide a subconscious context to the viewer of your actual words.

People need your nonverbal cues to understand your words.

How is this so?

"I'm not that intuitive or cool," you say.

But if I walked up to you smiling and said in a loud voice "GREAT to see you!" would you be prepared for an embrace or a handshake? You would know that the nonverbal cues (loud voice, smile, walking toward you) were emphasizing the words being spoken. In turn, you would have subconsciously prepared for the inevitable hug or handshake.

Now if I had seen you, made eye contact, clenched a fist, and started running at you, I'm pretty sure you wouldn't have expected that hug.

You are started to get sold on this whole nonverbal communication thing (I could tell because I am reading your body language right now).

But you're wondering when you can use this to your little manipulative advantage?

Nice try.

When Do We Communicate Nonverbally?

We are always communicating nonverbally, so it's important to understand what people grab from our nonverbal cues.

Here are five key roles that nonverbal cues can play:

> **Repeating:** they can repeat the message the person is verbally making. Nodding or motioning in rhythm to what he or she is saying are examples.
> **Contradicting:** they can contradict a message the individual is trying to convey, such as telling your dog "Good dog!" in a harsh, loud tone.
> **Substituting:** they can substitute for a verbal message. For example, a person's eyes can often convey a far more vivid message than words.
> **Complementing:** they may add to or complement a verbal message. A boss who pats an employee on the back while giving praise can increase the impact of his message.

> **Accenting:** they may accent or underline a verbal message. Pounding the table, for example, can underline a message being simultaneously spoken.

Intuitively you already know these rules.

You whisper in church and raise your voice in a crowd. You inflect differently when you're excited than when you're down. You've heard the expression a picture is worth a thousand words and so you've even played Pictionary with your friends.

You have told your kids that actions speak louder than words. You have a keen sense of when your kids are actually listening to you simply by their head movements, their eye contact, and other nonverbal cues—they look away when they are bored or distracted (or when asked to clean their room) and lean in with an erect posture when they're interested and engaged.

You have substituted words for nonverbal cues (the middle finger) and complemented your words with nonverbal actions (squeezing someone tighter to tell them you love them).

And if you have a "unique" uncle that comes over for Thanksgiving, you've accented your verbal messaging with some throwing-up of your hands in exasperation.

Second Date? Probably Not . . .

One of my friends is *really* into online dating (that is code language for he has gone on a lot of dates and had very little success keeping anyone interested). He's a great guy or I wouldn't call him a friend.

But this doesn't make him good at communication.

The other day I went out to a local coffee shop to get what Californians get at a coffee shop—something free trade, organic, fair sourced, and expensive—but really good.

For me that's actually green tea.

My friend, Mr. Online Dating Guy X, sat down with me after ordering. About thirty seconds into our conversation he started looking at his iPhone. His leg appeared restless. He looked over whenever the door opened and a couple walked in. With relative ease he came in and out of our conversation before going back to his iPhone to send a text.

I asked Mr. Online Dating Guy X how the whole online dating thing was going.

"Went on a date last weekend," he said, "but haven't heard back about another date."

Hmm . . . wonder why.

If his nonverbal cues at the coffee shop were anything like what he is giving off on dates it's not hard to see why date #2 is difficult to come by. He may be funny, he may be attractive. He may have even thought he was engaging on that date. But it's likely that most of what he was communicating was disinterest.

Because it's not what he would have said that night, it's what his date would have felt. And what she would have felt is what she would have *actually heard* no matter what he said. She would've felt 100 percent through his nonverbal cues that he had something better to do than to be there.

Jeanne Segal, author of *The Language of Emotional Intelligence,* has argued that the most powerful forms of communication occur *without* words at a *faster rate* than speech occurs.

Below the surface we are actually observing communication (nonverbal) and hearing communication (verbal). The glue, as she calls it, that holds the entire communication process together is the emotional exchange triggered by biologic reactions (such as fear, happiness, sadness).

How is most of this emotional exchange triggered?

Through nonverbal communication.

Nonverbal communication attracts the consumer of your information to have an emotional connection with you. Greater emotional connection equates to greater communication success.

Quite simply, it could eliminate the disconnect between your intent and what the recipient heard.

In Mr. Online Dating Guy's case, his nonverbal cues were sending signals of striking out much faster than his words could have done.

TV and The 24-Hour Talent Show

Nonverbal communication isn't just for online dating.

It has become a memorable part of political folklore.

Communications professor Randall Harrison showed how television first became a factor in the national scene during the 1948 election between Harry Truman and Thomas Dewey. Although television access at the time was limited mostly to the Northeast, the Democratic convention broadcast allowed voters to see Truman adopt a strong civil rights platform.

The cameras caught some of the Southern delegates walking out of the convention in response to hearing Truman's platform. Some have argued that this nonverbal visual, broadcast to thousands for the first time, helped mobilize voters in favor of Truman and possibly tipped the election in his favor.

As television expanded in its national reach and popularity, it became an integral medium for political and business communication. And most of what is communicated on TV within this arena is not from words but from the nonverbal cues that candidates or business executives give off. How often do you hear that "Candidate Jones just *looked* presidential?" Or, "the CEO of XYZ Company on TV looked like someone I could trust."

Not a peep about what Candidate Jones said or stands for or the CEO's capabilities to run the corporation.

The most powerful illustration of this visual television influence was on September 26, 1960, when nearly seventy million Americans watched the first televised general election debate—the Kennedy/Nixon debate.

You didn't have to be there to know who won on TV.

Kennedy.

And on radio?

Nixon.

Their debate results have been communicated so much as fact that it's hard not to believe them. Well, it turns out research done by David L. Vancil and Sue D. Pendell shows that no empirical evidence supports the conclusions of who won on television.

But it doesn't really matter. Facts are so passé.

What we can really glean from this debate illustration are two key points: the power of nonverbal communication and the power of the narrative.

Kennedy's performance, shown by audience responses to portray him as strong, sharp, relaxed, calm, and wise, led many to believe that this was the turning point for the campaign. The same audience responses showed Nixon as dull, weak, tense, and agitated.

Not good when you're trying to look "presidential."

More important, the TV debate played well into Kennedy's narrative as the candidate best able to lead the country into the "New Frontier" and played strongly against the narrative that Nixon was attempting to establish: that he was the experienced and able candidate.

Even though facts don't back up the conventional wisdom of who "won" the debate on radio and TV, this example demonstrates the power of what is being nonverbally communicated through images. Viewers use TV's extensive nonverbal cues to determine the effectiveness of a candidate's message. And who won the 1960 debate is so commonly accepted as fact further shows our underlying acceptance of the power of nonverbal cues.

Style became substance.

The same is true in business.

Akio Toyoda, president of Toyota, traveled to the United States in 2010 to speak in front of Congress after a series of high-profile crashes and recalls attacked their brand. He offered the following apology:

"I extend my condolences from the deepest part of my heart. . . . I am deeply sorry for any accidents that Toyota drivers have experienced. Especially, I would like to extend my condolences . . . for the accident in San Diego. I would like to send my prayers again, and I will do everything in my power to ensure that such a tragedy never happens again."

Pretty straightforward, right? Sounds like he said the right things.

But Congresswoman Marcy Kaptur said during the testimony that she was "disappointed" with Toyoda's testimony and did not feel he had shown sufficient remorse. Her statements, and sentiment, were repeated by dozens of news outlets that night.

Why did they draw this conclusion?

Because Toyoda "appeared too calm" or "too relaxed." He needed to show more "true remorse."

These were comments provided by media outlets and political commentators.

During Akio Toyoda's testimony, many thought he did not strike the proper "tone." Consequently, it didn't matter what he said.

Many believed, fairly or unfairly, that he failed at his communication simply because his nonverbal "words" were heard differently from his *actual* words.

How we are perceived nonverbally is becoming even more important in the modern world of technology. Today, viewers are barraged with visuals that highlight our nonverbal communication skills (or lack thereof). Every action is caught on tape and posted on YouTube; every gesture is repeated in tabloids, in the blogosphere, and on twenty-four-hour cable channels.

Akio Toyoda learned this the hard way. His demeanor was replayed on cable channels and online right alongside his actual words.

In fact, his words weren't even the focus of the talking heads—just his demeanor was.

All of this speaks to the reality that nonverbal cues will provide a great deal of information to your target audience and are even more relevant now that visual information is so readily accessible.

So how do you use this for your business?

It's important when you're making presentations, collaborating with co-workers, or even negotiating to think about what your nonverbal cues are saying.

As Carol Kinsey Goman points out in her book on nonverbal communication, *The Silent Language of Leaders*, people gravitate toward leaders who show warmth and authority. You can communicate warmth nonverbally, she says, with "open body postures, palm-up hand gestures . . . positive eye contact, head nods and smiles." Similar to Mayor Giuliani, you can show authority with posture and command of physical space and voice.

In the case of Akio Toyoda, however, his nonverbal cues did not give off the warmth or authority that made his words believable. He failed to connect emotionally with his audience and as a result many felt that his words fell flat.

Goman provides many examples of how one of the greatest determinants to success, in politics, business, or interpersonal communications, is this feeling of emotional connection through warmth and authority. It provides a trust and believability factor that is hard to beat.

In fact, your audience will determine this connection using mostly nonverbal cues in a very short period of time.

Psychologists Nalini Ambady and Robert Rosenthal conducted experiments on what they deem "thin slices of expressive behavior." These micro-exposures to people, sometimes thirty seconds or less, create opinions that almost exclusively rely on nonverbal elements.

In one study, noted by Goman, "subjects watched a thirty-second clip of college teachers at the beginning of a term and rated them on such characteristics as accepting, active, competent and confident."

With this small sample of data, these raters were "able to accurately predict how students would evaluate those same teachers at the end of the course."

Judgments are being made by your audience within seconds of you entering the room. What nonverbal cues you give off during the introduction and throughout your presentation, collaboration, or negotiation will leave a lasting impression. This impression can be positive (Mayor Giuliani) or not (Mr. Online Dating Guy X).

To be fair, in Mr. Online Dating Guy X's case, his date would have had him pretty much figured out the second he went for his iPhone.

For Akio Toyoda, his nonverbal cues (mainly in tone) led Congressional leaders and others to write off his actual words quite quickly, which, unfortunately for him, established a story that focused less on what he had said and more on how he had said it.

Now Go Do It

Now you have an idea of why it's important to pay attention to what you're saying without words. But you're left wondering, "So what are some tricks of nonverbal communication?"

Here is a short list of four main elements of nonverbal communication. If you can genuinely maintain awareness of these elements, your message will be received in the way it was intended.

1. **Facial Expressions:** As obvious as it may seem, facial expressions have a strong impact on how people interpret your message. Think about the power of a genuine smile or the softening of your expressions (note the key word genuine, you are not looking for a Joan Rivers smile here). You can quickly diffuse a difficult situation with a genuine facial expression or help ease a room with a sincere look. How often have you developed a loyal relationship with a local news station because the anchor had a "trusted" or "familiar" face? How about the opposite? Or have you ever sat on a jury and felt that the witness could be trusted? Or maybe the witness was lying? Chances are you don't have personal knowledge of the witness, but his face *told* you all you needed to know.

2. **Voice:** You don't have to be Pavarotti to experience the power of pitch, volume, tibre, and rhythm. Musicians, great communicators, and moms everywhere do it instinctively. Think about it. When you want to communicate effectively with your kid, your boss, or your spouse, you will adjust the pitch and volume naturally. Taking it to the next step, think back to a memorable speech you've heard, maybe Martin Luther King, Jr.'s "I Have a Dream" speech. Think about the rhythm and repetition of the line "I have a dream." You can hear it in your head—you can hear as he increases volume on points that are important, alters pitch, and builds a rhythm that is so methodical it helps you *remember* the words. His voice helps you draw an emotional connection with the words and it helps you feel the words on a greater level .

3. **Eye Contact:** Most people are visual people. After all, how often have you heard someone describe the beauty of Hawaii exclusively by sound? Given the dominance of the visual sense, it is only logical that how you look at someone can communicate specific things. You instinctively know that eye contact is essential to showing interest or affection or even hostility. Remember your kid's failing to tell you the truth? Eyes not looking at you, right? Lovers look longingly into their partner's eyes to show love (maybe just puppy love) while po-

lice investigators may look straight at a suspect's eyes to show they mean business. How effective would a candidate be who didn't look directly at an interviewer? What about their giving a speech to hundreds of adoring fans while looking at the sky or ground? This is why teleprompters are clear and at eye-level—so the speaker can always be looking at and therefore connecting with the audience.

4. **Gestures:** The middle finger is not just for freeways. There are other effective gestures, too, although fans at Yankees vs. Red Sox games may disagree. When used correctly, gestures can be powerful. They can emphasize points or soften tone. They can be memorable; think President Clinton's usage of the pointing finger when he said, "I did not have sexual relations with that woman, Miss Lewinsky." And they can also be too memorable; the Village People's "Y.M.C.A.," anyone? Sorry about getting that song in your head, but at least I know you are visualizing those gestures right now.

Remember, nonverbal and verbal communication are always connected. So when you are going to give a boardroom presentation or deliver your core message in front of an audience, be mindful of what you're communicating nonverbally. Think through the four nonverbal elements—facial expressions, voice, eye contact, and gestures—before you deliver your message. If you use these elements, your core message will be received in the best light possible.

CHAPTER 4

BRANDING

The Recall

Let's say your CFO comes to you with a slight dilemma.

Sales are down 36 percent, your product is under multiple recalls, you are facing millions of dollars of lawsuits, and Congress has just asked the company president to testify.

Would you tell her not to worry? That, after all, sales will rebound in two short years and that your brand is so strong that damage will be fleeting?

You wouldn't unless you were the CEO of Toyota.

This was exactly what Toyota was facing in 2009. The company, built on a brand of reliability, was now recalling nearly 4 million cars because of potential floor mat and accelerator issues.

But two short years later the automaker's sales had recovered and the brand was still intact.

Why?

Because Toyota has invested in something beyond a simple marketing plan. They have invested in their narrative and brand.

Think about it. When you think "Toyota" what comes to mind?

Perhaps it is their Toyota Production System, where anyone on the assembly line can halt production by noticing a single flaw? Or if you're like me you had no idea that such a thing existed but you knew that one thing was synonymous with Toyota's brand: reliability.

This isn't accidental.

Sure, there is truth to the reliability of their vehicles and their oft-cited production program. But what's just as important is the fact that they chose to construct this as their narrative and then built a brand around it.

Mike Stefaniak, a marketing professional, says there is a difference between simply marketing products or policies and actually investing in creating a brand for the company.

"Strong company reputations can contribute to the product being a safe choice," he explained to *Industry Week* magazine. "Many [companies] have traditionally focused on selling and marketing products versus also selling and marketing the company. The result: They tend to lose the means of creating the customer interest that ultimately leads to product loyalty."

Toyota took a long-term approach and invested in the concept of a reliable company.

So why would this matter?

When the brand was under attack during the recalls of tens of thousands of vehicles the strength of their narrative carried them through. The stories about vehicle unreliability and safety were incongruous with what people believed to be true.

This doesn't mean that Toyota didn't suffer. Obviously their sales dropped by 36 percent. But it does mean that they were able to weather it in the long run because their narrative and brand beat out the short-term story.

A Picture, Place or Thing?

Just what exactly is branding?

According to Matthew Healey, author of *What Is Branding*, the word "brand" comes from the Germanic root meaning "burn."

Makes sense.

When I travel through eastern Colorado to visit family I've met plenty of cattle that have learned the root word of "brand" is "burn."

But clearly it has a more figurative usage when we're talking about companies or political candidates. Unlike cattle, the brand isn't simply used to show ownership of something, but to figuratively talk about the impression you or your product leaves in your customer's mind.

So how do we define branding?

Patrick Barwise wrote a collection of essays for *The Economist* entitled *Brands and Branding,* and he defined three distinct things a brand can be:

> ➤ A named product or service, such as Toyota, Ivory Soap, or the BBC News. This refers to the branded product or service itself.
> ➤ A trademark such as Panasonic or Target, referring to the name or symbol
> ➤ A customer's beliefs about a product or service

The third component, "a customer's beliefs" is the most important and the following examples will illustrate why.

As Matthew Healey notes in his book, a brand is a promise of satisfaction. While your audience or consumers can form their own feelings about what a brand mean.s, they can be influenced by the work of the manufacturer, company, or individual that is trying to define its brand.

Each year in the United States alone companies invest nearly half a trillion dollars on marketing their goods and services. A good portion of this is spent on bringing new products to the market—yet most of these new products and services fail.

Many of these companies feel they are investing in their "brand" despite the chance of failure. What they are really doing, however, is investing in the advertising industry.

Successful brands are more than just a symbol or product; they connect with the user. They cannot be created with advertising alone or only with catchy slogans. To be successful a brand needs to create a positive user association.

Have you ever wondered why everyone knows the logo for Target and Nike but most would be hard pressed to describe the logo for US Air? Or why certain products, like Apple, carry a cachet not found with their competitors?

These brands worked to create strong symbols, narratives, and emotional connections that allowed customers to experience their products on multiple levels.

It turns out there is some fancy science behind this.

Dr. Antonio Damasio, a professor of neuroscience at the University of Southern California, developed a concept he dubbed the somatic marker hypothesis. His hypothesis, that decisions are made with both cognitive and emotional processes, can be applied to help explain how brands resonate with consumers.

As Erik du Plessis explains in *The Advertised Mind,* more information flows from the area of emotion in the brain toward the area of rationality than the other way around. For example, when researchers interview respondents and ask, "What do you think of . . . " their answer will invariably be "I like it, because . . ." or "I don't like it, because . . ." The answer the respondent gives, du Plessis explains, is the emotional reaction first followed by the rationalization of it.

In other words, your audience has an emotional response first and rationalizes that response. To have an impact, brands need to connect emotionally. They need to find a way to put the audience at the center and humanize the experience so it resonates.

Let's look at some examples.

Being the Cool Kid

Last year my wife decided she had enough of my cursing at the computer.

It seemed that every time I started my trusty laptop up it would freeze, shut down, or claim that I had won a million dollars in a totally legit foreign lottery.

Unfortunately I was never able to claim my money because my computer wouldn't stay on long enough for it to be relevant.

I like to think of myself as tech-savvy. This means I'm not but it doesn't matter because I'm branding myself as such right now. My wife, however, is tech-savvy. And she told me that if I wanted a reliable computer I would have to get a Mac.

So as we drove twenty-five minutes to the Apple Store, I was thinking about the possibilities for my new laptop. It had been quite some time since I had owned a Mac. In fact, the last Mac I owned had one of those rainbow colored logos and a green screen.

I knew that Macs were for the cool kids. You know, the cool kid sitting next to you on the flight with the noise-canceling headphones and the architectural-design software program?

Those kids.

But I hadn't really thought about why I accepted this as fact.

Had anyone done any reliability studies? Were there coolness studies done on kids to see what computers they owned?

Or was Apple quietly doing something that we weren't attuned to: building their narrative and brand?

In the late 1980s Apple hired a big-time marketing executive named John Sculley. Sculley was fresh off of making Pepsi so ubiquitous that anyone now can see the logo when asleep.

At Apple, Sculley did what any good marketer would do: he increased the marketing budget seven-fold. But the money he spent on marketing was less important than building an already budding narrative about the brand.

A small, committed group of loyal users had a true emotional connection to the product. This small group was laying the groundwork for the narrative about Apple, which would define their brand. Sculley, and others at Apple, knew that the marketing would simply complement the development of this narrative.

Want to be innovative?

You have to own an Apple product.

Think anyone will like you on campus with that Dell? Think again!

Apple's narrative was one of new, innovative products. They were outside of the mainstream. They were the brand with which you could "Think Different."

Marc Gobe, author of *Emotional Branding*, puts it more bluntly.

"Without the brand, Apple would be dead," he said. "Absolutely. Completely. The brand is all they've got. The power of their branding is all that keeps them alive. It's got nothing to do with products."

In the 1990s Sculley was forced out and the company was in complete turmoil. Apple's board of directors went on a firing spree and it seemed like the company was done. But a movement was afoot to save the company; not just by the board and shareholders, but the small group of loyal users.

When the floundering company was taken over by Steve Jobs, its best remaining asset was this narrative and budding brand. The company began to build on this narrative and create an emotional connection with its users.

In fact, Apple knew that the loyalty of these users would drive sales. Through word of mouth, innovation, and simple uniqueness, Apple would build an emotional connection and establish loyalty with its users.

In many ways, the design and marketing of Apple is "people-driven."

If you can genuinely connect with people's hopes and aspirations, if you can create this emotional connection, you can establish a narrative and brand that will endure. And just as important, you will create something that will help inoculate you when things aren't going so well, as was evident with Toyota.

Bestselling author and columnist Naomi Klein notes that people are drawn to brands like Apple "because they are selling their own ideas back to them, they are selling the most powerful ideas that we have in our culture such as transcendence and community."

So what exactly did Apple do to create a successful brand?

Apple has embraced three key elements that have made their brand endure, all of which are essential to ensuring your brand succeeds:

1. They created an emotionally connected product.
2. They designed a logo that is easy to remember and instantly recognizable.
3. They humanized the experience.

Thinking back to what a brand is (a named product, a trademark or logo, and a customer's beliefs), you can see that Apple hits the target on multiple fronts. They created a strong narrative about the company that put user experience at the front end. Users became emotionally connected to their products, which helped develop a "brand" of Apple—of one that the kids with the noise-canceling headphones would use.

To top it off their logo is relevant and instantly recognizable.

Now the strength of the brand is so obvious that there are hundreds of websites dedicated to Apple's products and storyline.

When will the new iPhone or iPad be released?

What does it look like?

We've heard that it has a new four-inch display, camera, and features that put it at the top of its class!

The same isn't true for computer companies with weaker brands.

Trust me, people aren't clamoring over the release of the next [insert non-Apple brand here] computer.

The strength of Apple's brand has led to a gain of immeasurable amounts of free advertising, from the hundreds of blogs dedicated to them and media outlets clamoring to have an inside scoop on new releases, and even more word-of-mouth advertising from the cool kids.

This brand strength leads people to purchase the product *just to show* other people they own the product.

As crazy as it may sound, a number of our brand purchases are made to show others that we are cool enough to have that brand.

Reading the *Wall Street Journal* or *New York Times* while on the subway?

Brainiac.

Sipping the $4 (on sale) Starbucks latte with the big green logo on the cup?

Cooler than diner coffee.

Working on your silver Apple Macbook while on the plane?

Way cooler than your seatmate's Dell.

As public relations guru Joe Marconi notes, research has confirmed that a "significant number of people make their final purchase decisions in virtually every product category, from their daily newspapers to their . . . cars based [on] considerations of image and reputation." In other words, consumers buy based on how they will look to their peers and even to strangers.

This is the power of brands like Apple.

And they all create this type of brand by hitting on the three key elements: emotional connection, being instantly recognizable, and humanizing the experience (giving a customer-centric experience).

It's easy to see how this works. What companies do you instantly recognize? Target? Nike? Maybe Starbucks or Calvin Klein?

All have hit on those three key elements. Even the Obama Campaign succeeded on these three fronts.

But as we've previously discussed, it isn't simply about creating a brand, as there is an underlying narrative that reinforces these brands.

Apple worked hard to create the narrative about a company that put user experience at the front end. Users became emotionally connected to their products, which in turn helped develop the "brand."

Growing Hair After a Divorce

So you're in your twenties and you're going through a divorce. You look in the mirror, notice a receding hairline and think that your options on the bar scene are pretty slim.

What do you do?

If you're Sy Sperling, you build an empire called Hair Club for Men.

Hair Club for Men has fiercely loyal customers. Similar to Apple, Hair Club's connection with the customers has allowed the company to weather rough patches and grow.

How much growth? A few years ago the company sold for more than $200 million.

But how did Sperling do it?

Let's be honest, this isn't exactly an idea that you run to venture capitalists about. But in the late 1970s when Sperling was creating the company, the hair replacement options were slim.

Hair plugs? No chance.

Toupee? Your options on the bar scene would be even slimmer.

So the need was there. But how did Sperling develop the trust, connection, and narrative that allowed for a $200 million company?

"I'm not only the Hair Club president, I'm also a client."

With this personalized outlook Sperling focused on three key elements that allowed him to create his brand.

> ➤ He created an emotionally connected product.
> ➤ He built a tagline that was instantly recognizable.
> ➤ He put the audience at the center of the story and humanized the experience.

EMOTIONAL CONNECTION	INSTANTLY RECOGNIZABLE	HUMANIZED EXPERIENCE
Getting divorced and need some hair? Well, Hair Club provided a viable solution to a difficult, and often-emotional situation. "I knew how my product made me feel, and I knew that other people wanted to feel [that] way," Sperling noted.	You couldn't go anywhere without seeing those TV ads mentioning "I'm not only the Hair Club president, I'm also a client." Yes, those commercials were made fun of, but, boy, were they ever recognizable. Simply repeat that quote to someone and they will know it equals Hair Club.	"We used real people in all our advertising and marketing," Sperling says. "The company had terrific growth because people could see that they were just like the people in our ads." The company made the product real and relevant to its audience. The brand then became one of authenticity.

Erika Napoletano, a social media and branding expert, used Hair Club for Men as an example of what entrepreneurs should aim for when creating a business. Hair Club, she said succeeded in large part because it connected with its target audience. "When you know your audience, you can use that information to grow your business—even if customers aren't going to run out and tell their best friend about it."

Sperling noted that he built a client-centric product. The brand flowed from that. "I listened to what they wanted," he said; "they repaid me by becoming loyal customers."

Swoosh This

When we were younger my brothers and I could not afford the cool shoes. The cool shoes being those pumped-up kicks that were made by Nike—the Air Jordan.

Our mother, always the innovator, took us to the discount shoe store to pick up other shoes that had the same ability to be "pumped" at about 10 percent of the price.

Instead of a swoosh logo the shoes had an orange basketball and no brand name. I loved them and promptly ruined them like all growing boys do to new things their mothers buy for them.

Looking back on it those shoes looked ridiculous. But for some reason, Nike had made those shoes (and the knock-offs we wore) relevant to society.

But why is it that Nike, and specifically the swoosh logo, resonate? How is it that $35, the price paid to a Portland State University arts student to design the logo, transformed a brand?

Well, initially the swoosh didn't resonate. As Robert Goldman, author of *Nike Culture,* has written, the swoosh logo was originally described by customers as a "fat checkmark."

I can see that.

But, as Goldman reveals, the logo acquired "meaning and value through repeated association with other culturally meaningful symbols." In other words, Nike worked to create a business culture that allowed consumers to develop an emotional connection with their products and Nike to brand a lifestyle as much as a product.

How did they do that?

First, Nike created a tagline "Just Do It" that had a strong connection to the individual. Consumers could see that they were at the center of the brand and narrative. The tagline spoke to individual empowerment and connected nicely with the underlying expectation that working out was about the individual.

Second, they focused their advertising on relevant pop culture elements. Nike has always gone beyond the connection of celebrity athlete endorsers to put the consumer front and center in the narrative. They believe their audience is culturally savvy and media literate, so they draw on advertising elements that support these qualities.

Nike made themselves culturally relevant and engaged consumers in popular frameworks they could easily understand.

Nike's brand was built on the overall attitude they project. As Robert Goldman points out, Nike ads connect the Nike brand attitude and voice with the viewer's sense of identity (Just Do It). The ads build an emotional connection with the viewer in which the viewer believes he or she is part of the brand.

Let's break down the three key components of the Nike brand:

EMOTIONAL CONNECTION	INSTANTLY RECOGNIZABLE	HUMANIZED EXPERIENCE
Nike established their brand as culturally relevant. They engage consumers in popular frameworks (sports, music, culture) that are immediately understood. People connect to their products because their products are relevant to the times.	The swoosh logo is everywhere—from shoes to clothing to luggage and cologne. It is hard to escape the logo in sports, in advertising or even at the gym. They have developed a simple logo that speaks to the brand.	"Just Do It," the Nike tagline, speaks to self-empowerment. The audience is at the center of their brand and narrative. The narrative and tagline allows the individual to take control of his or her own destiny.

Nike's ability to resonate as both a brand and cultural symbol has helped them develop consumer loyalty and strong market share. Think about some of their competitors—Reebok and New Balance. It's much harder to envision the logos of those brands, know their taglines, or know even the degree to which their products exist in the marketplace (does New Balance make luggage?).

Branding the Politicos

When it comes to branding, what is true in business is often true in politics as well.

Political campaigns have taken a number of cues from the advertising world. In fact, it's not uncommon for candidates to work with corporate branding experts to help establish everything from their logo to their image.

Candidates with strong narratives, emotional connections, and visual representations such as logos build the strongest brands. But is branding an individual different from branding a business?

In many ways, no.

Over time elected officials and political parties work to establish a narrative and a brand. Just like a business trying to sell something, campaigns and politicians use these building blocks to frame messages and convince voters to "buy" them.

No pun intended.

Just how does a candidate create a brand?

Well, one unsuccessful way to do it, unless you like to lose, is purely through data. Facts and figures are great unless that's all you give people.

How often have you seen a person inspired to tell their neighbors to vote for someone after a candidate gave a riveting speech about the inner workings of the GDP or the deficit? Other than my former finance professor I think the answer is never.

But many individuals still attempt to brand themselves exclusively through knowledge and not through personal connection.

Successful businesses, however, inherently understand the importance of personal connection. For example, let's look at Apple again. They have created products that run on incredibly complex back-end systems but provide products that most would say are extremely easy to use. Apple isn't marketing the complexity of their technical knowledge or the depth of their products' systems, they are marketing the simplicity to the end user.

So why do political types like to be the smartest person in the room, and show it?

Political scientist Michael Jones, who studies narrative in politics, said it well: "[Some politicians] are stuck in this Enlightenment reasoning kind of thing, thinking that if you take the facts to people about a particular policy it will be enough. . . . It's this idea that you just present better information and you get better policy outcomes."

But it doesn't quite work that way.

Similar to a business, individuals create a successful brand by engaging people, connecting, and allowing their audience to see themselves as part of the solution.

Let's take a look at some successful political brands with different political stripes: Ronald Reagan and Barack Obama.

Running for reelection Ronald Reagan first appeared at the 1984 Republican National Convention, on a screen above a stage. The stage had a podium flanked by two American flags; the convention hall—a collection of red, white, and blue—was adorned with images of the president.

As Tim Raphael, a professor at Rutgers, wrote in his article "The Reagan Brand" (appearing in *The President Electric*), "as political theater, the performance embodied an intricate network of connections between statecraft and stagecraft, culture and capital."

Ronald Reagan, he noted, was the product of an exhaustive education in the performance techniques and technologies spawned by radio, film, and television. He knew how to establish his story and build his brand as the "great communicator."

But how did Reagan create this brand?

Reagan worked to create a strong narrative of conservative values, limited government, and optimism in America. Through vivid imagery, "Morning Again in America" and "America is Back" campaign commercials, he created an emotional connection to what *it felt like* to live in Reagan's America.

Reagan reinforced this narrative through everything he presented: press conferences, speeches, slogans, and even surrogates speaking on his behalf. Once he had the strong narrative publicly established, the Reagan "brand" was easy to create.

He employed a full-court press of story, casting, and marketing that has created a brand that endures even decades after his presidency. Ultimately, Reagan was able to hit on the three key elements of branding:

➤ He created an emotional connection with his audience.
➤ He built an image that was instantly recognizable.
➤ He put the audience at the center of the story.

EMOTIONAL CONNECTION	INSTANTLY RECOGNIZABLE	HUMANIZED EXPERIENCE
Reagan worked to show a vision of what it felt like to live in Reagan's America. Reinforced through advertising, speeches, and even his campaign slogan "It's morning in America," Reagan created a brand that he hoped voters would equate with optimism, strength, and self-determination.	Reagan as an individual was ubiquitous. As Tim Raphael notes, he was on the network news, performing roles in old movies or plugging new ones, emceeing all-star galas, or speaking with Charlton Heston at a tribute or with Vin Scully as guest commentator at a Dodgers' game.	Reagan's speeches put the audience at the center of the story, including at his first Inaugural: "I could say 'you' and 'your' because I am addressing the heroes of whom I speak—you, the citizens of this blessed land. Your dreams, your hopes, your goals are going to be the dreams, the hopes, and the goals of this administration."

In 2004 a relatively unknown candidate for the United States Senate with an unusual name gave the keynote address at the Democratic National Convention. Four years later, he was president.

Barack Obama built a brand that allowed him to win a senate seat, beat better-known and better-funded opponents in a presidential primary, and then ascend to the highest office in the United States. All in less time than it takes some people to obtain their PhD.

But how did he build his brand in such a short time?

Through an emotionally compelling narrative.

In 2004, when Barack Obama first burst onto the national scene, the country was mired in two wars, the terrorist actions of September 11th were fresh in the country's mind, and political polarization appeared to be reaching its peak. In the four years between his famous 2004 speech and his announcement for his presidential bid, things had gotten worse.

Obama wasn't out of central casting for this position. Born to interracial parents in Hawaii (a state that had never had one of its own become president), and having lived and been schooled for much of his childhood in a foreign country, he didn't exactly meet the standard criteria.

This, in many ways, would prove the basis for his narrative and brand. The country was ready for a change and the best change agent was one that didn't come from the traditional mold. Obama wove deeply personal stories about his family, upbringing, personal struggles, and international experiences into his public narrative.

He embodied change and the hope for something better: those were his key narrative elements.

Similar to Reagan, Obama reinforced his narrative through everything he presented: press conferences, speeches, slogans, and surrogates. His campaign slogan was "change" and his logo was designed to resemble a sun rising. Thus, he built his brand on this narrative.

Let's look at the key elements:

EMOTIONAL CONNECTION	INSTANTLY RECOGNIZABLE	HUMANIZED EXPERIENCE
Obama worked to develop direct emotional connections with his audience. His brand was to have the audience become part of the "change" narrative. He reinforced this connection speeches, advertising, surrogates, and his campaign slogan.	Obama's logo, and presence, became synonymous with his narrative. His logo, resembling a rising sun, represented the change as a new dawn. He did interviews on sports networks, family programming, and more to reinforce the narrative that the audience was the "change."	Obama's speeches put the audience at the center of the story. "You know, they said this day would never come. They said our sights were set too high. They said this country was too divided, too disillusioned to ever come together around a common purpose. But on this ... night, at this defining moment in history, you have done what the cynics said we couldn't do. You said the time has come to move beyond the bitterness and pettiness and anger that's consumed Washington. ... We're choosing unity over division, and sending a powerful message that change is coming to America."

Mickey D's

Some brands are happy with sales in the hundreds. McDonald's enjoys rocking the billions.

But how did a fifty-two-year-old milkshake-machine salesman turn McDonald's into one of the world's most preeminent brands?

Ray Kroc was a fairly successful milkshake-machine salesman. As part of his job he would regularly visit clients throughout the country and one set of clients in particular, Maurice and Richard McDonald, caught his eye.

The McDonald brothers were born in New Hampshire but had visions of leaving the East to make it big in Hollywood. So they packed up their things and gave Tinseltown a try. Because you and everyone you know has eaten at a McDonald's I think you know how their acting careers panned out. But they did just fine doing what most Los Angeles actors and actresses actually do to make a living: working in food service.

The brothers eventually opened up a drive-in restaurant in San Bernardino, about fifty miles east of Los Angeles. As Daniel Gross, author of *Forbes Greatest Business Stories of All Time* tells it, Ray Kroc was fascinated with the high-volume of milkshake-machine orders coming out of this drive-in.

While most restaurants owned one or two Prince Castle Multi-Mixers, which could crank out five shakes at once, the McDonald brothers owned eight—providing the capacity to mix forty shakes at once.

So Kroc headed out to San Bernardino to see what kind of operation the brothers were running.

"Kroc stood in the shadows of the stand's two radiant golden arches, which lit up the sky at dusk, and saw lines of people snaking outside the octagonal restaurant," Gross noted. "Through the building's all-glass walls, he watched the male crew, clad in white paper hats and white uniforms, hustle about the squeaky-clean restaurant, dishing out burgers, fries, and shakes to the working-class families that drove up."

Ray Kroc knew something big was happening here. He saw the

making of a brand and asked the brothers about franchising. After working out the details, Kroc set about on his new endeavor: overseeing the franchising of McDonald's.

There were challenges to building the new brand.

How could he differentiate McDonald's from the other players in the business (such as A&W, Dairy Queen, and Big Boy)?

How could he provide a product that customers could rely on?

How could he get disparate franchise owners to buy into the philosophy of McDonald's so they could succeed just like the San Bernardino restaurant did?

How could he draw the emotional connection, develop a brand that was recognizable, and put the customers at the front of the experience—all necessary signs of a successful brand?

To build the McDonald's brand, Kroc knew that he had to impose discipline on the loosely run restaurant industry. This would be a key component of the success of McDonald's: standardization.

So Kroc developed standardized-operating procedures into easily replicable processes. He believed that there was a similar science to making a hamburger as there was to making a car on an assembly line.

"Kroc endowed his beef patties with exacting specifications—fat content: below 19 percent; weight: 1.6 ounces; diameter: 3.875 inches; onions: 1/4 ounce. Kroc even built a laboratory in suburban Chicago to devise a method for making the perfect fried potato in the late 1950s," notes Gross.

None of the other chains adhered to this type of strict standardization. This allowed customers to be able to rely on the McDonald's product, a key differentiation between McDonald's and other growing chains.

As Gross points out, this meant that McDonald's became a chain "in which a store in Delaware and a store in Nevada could serve burgers of the exact same size and quality, each containing the same number of pickle slices and topped with the same-size dollops of mustard and ketchup, each arrayed on a similar tray alongside potatoes deep-fried for the exact same length of time."

The McDonald's brand to the customer became one of reliability and consistency—you knew when you went there, regardless of where you were in the country, what you were going to get.

Feel free to count the pickles on your next Mickey D's burger. Expect to have two.

And beyond the kitchen, Kroc standardized uniforms (white), design of shops (the golden arches), and menu prices. These aspects of his standardization also helped differentiate McDonald's from other chains and develop an instantly recognizable product for the customer.

But Ray Kroc still needed to ensure that franchisees would buy in to this model. As he said, "My belief was that I had to help the individual operator succeed in every way I could. His success would insure my success. But I couldn't do that and, at the same time, treat him as a customer."

So this led to his last critical component of building a successful brand: he created an emotional connection with the franchisees.

He viewed all of the franchisees as business partners, not as mere customers. They weren't simply there to purchase frozen potatoes and milkshake machines, they were there to buy into the McDonald's philosophy: consistent products, prices, and experiences.

As Kroc noted, he was selling his business partners an operating system: a branded service. "Perfection is very difficult to achieve, and perfection was what I wanted in McDonald's." Kroc said. "Our aim, of course, was to ensure repeat business based on the system's reputation rather than on the quality of a single store or operator."

By getting operators to buy into this standardized process he knew that he could build the brand's reputation. Fifty years later the McDonald's brand still stands strong.

Let's look at how McDonald's approached the three key elements of branding.

EMOTIONAL CONNECTION	INSTANTLY RECOGNIZABLE	HUMANIZED EXPERIENCE
Ray Kroc viewed franchisees as business partners, not just customers. This let franchisees buy into his branded system as equals. The more they felt connected to the system, the more they became evangelists for the brand. Growth depended on the franchisees' personal emotional connection to the McDonald's brand.	McDonald's became the most standardized operation in the food industry. From the golden arches outside to the white-uniformed employees, hamburgers, and fries inside, you knew whether you were eating in Des Moines or Los Angeles that you were getting the same recognizable fare. Customers could and still can easily recognize the brand and what it signifies.	Kroc recognized that customers' experiences would ultimately drive sales. Kids were encouraged through Happy Meals and jungle gyms; parents were rewarded with inexpensive food and consistent experiences. Going to McDonald's became an experience: one that customers knew what to expect even before they saw the golden arches.

I Asked for a Beer

Some brands fail because they fail to develop an emotional connection with the end user.

Some are just bad ideas.

In 1990 Coors decided it should enter the water business.

Technically, it was already in the water business since it had been brewing its iconic American lager with Rocky Mountain spring water for more than 100 years.

Hoping to capitalize on the growth of the bottled water market, Coors introduced Rocky Mountain Sparkling Water—complete with the famous Coors logo on the center of the label.

They should have seen that this was a bad idea. Imagine your child walking up to a store cooler and picking up some Coors water. "Don't worry mom, the buzz wears off really fast!"

Within a short period, the product flopped.

But did Rocky Mountain Sparkling Water have to fail?

Imagine if I presented you with this case study and asked for you to predict the success of a product:

A company is entering a market with established distribution, easy access to raw materials, loyal customers, universal brand recognition, and a consistent advertising and marketing program.

On top of it the company has millions of dollars in seed money to launch this product.

In addition, any new competitors interested in joining the market would need to spend millions on infrastructure to gain access to raw materials, would have to spend even more on advertising and distribution networks, and were most likely months from initial production.

Still think Rocky Mountain Sparkling Water would fail considering these advantages?

So what lessons can we take from Coors' water venture as to why brands fail? The key element lies in the narrative Coors had spent more than a hundred years building.

Since its inception Coors has developed a narrative of purity in its beer, "brewed with pure Rocky Mountain Spring Water."

Water was an input. It was what Coors claimed made the *beer* better.

Water, however, wasn't what defined Coors' brand—it was the beer that did.

When you spend more than a hundred years defining your name, logo, and brand as a beer company, it doesn't resonate when you become something else.

Coors had built their reputation, a time-tested, consistent, and predictable reputation, for being a beer company. In other words, Coors broke their brand promise the minute they left the beer business.

Think back to the case study.

Coors had a number of competitive advantages over their rivals and very possibly could have created a successful water brand. But they tried to build it off of something that didn't make sense to the consumer. In fact, they tried to build the water brand from something they had spent more than a hundred years showing that they weren't: a water brand.

What is the Logo for US Airways?

Most new products fail.

And many products in a category look or function in the exact same way, making it difficult for consumers to tell the difference.

So what makes a brand stick? Why are some logos more memorable than others? And just what *is* the logo for US Airways?

To spare you from Googling it and take away the suspense, the US Airways logo is a stylized version of American flag.

Why doesn't that logo stick in most consumers' minds?

Barry Silverstein, co-author of *The Breakaway Brand*, may have the answer: Major airline carriers have done little over the last few decades to differentiate themselves.

The major carriers tend to move as a unit as they set prices, establish routes, or eliminate food service. As a consequence, "their brands have become largely indistinguishable, with corporate colors, boarding passes and flight attendants' uniforms all looking alike."

US Airways, when it went through a rebranding in the late 1990s, repainted its planes to look similar to United Airlines' planes. They even ended up with a former United exec as their new chairman.

As US Airways became indistinguishable from their competition so too did their brand. Since the company wasn't really giving a unique identity to the public, the public couldn't identify the company.

With no distinction in the market it is hard for consumers to remember a logo. Brands stick when they can show they are different. From Starbucks to Apple, brands that built a connection and allowed the consumer to feel they were at the forefront of something different were able to run the field.

Think about airlines that have worked to break through this space—such as Southwest Airlines and JetBlue. Both have created strong narratives about being different and both have worked to brand themselves as being outside of the regular airline mold.

Unsurprisingly, both have by and large weathered the economic downturn much better than their indistinguishable competitors. And both have stronger brands than some of the legacy carriers like US Airways.

For example, Southwest Airlines flew nearly 128 million passengers in 2011 compared with 68 million for US Airways. And even Southwest's colors are significantly different from other airlines. As a consequence, they visually stand out at an airport; their color scheme, and also their design, has stronger recognition for consumers than US Airways.

The next time you are at an airport, look out at the runway. Can you instantly tell which airline is taking off in the distance? Can you distinguish the brands?

Brands that stick do so because every element about the brand, the narrative, the messaging, and the branding allow for differentiation and emotional connection to their service.

The US Airways example shows the direct relationship between branding and narrative. Their brand was indistinguishable, and their narrative wasn't strong enough for them to break away as a brand.

In many respects the airline worked to create a narrative that made them no different from other airlines—the same price, the same services, even the same routes. Fundamentally you could interchange their service with a number of other services. Not exactly something that would create brand loyalty. As a consequence, their brand, their logo, and even their profits suffered.

Let's compare their narrative to the Southwest story.

As alluded to earlier, Southwest's narrative is of a low fare airline, a fun airline—a willingness to do something different. As Kevin Freiberg wrote in his book about Southwest Airlines' success, they worked so hard to be different that they even chose to fly in and out of secondary airports in major markets.

The airline has been "innovative and unconventional in serving smaller airports where there is less congestion and less competition" such as Love Field in Dallas, Hobby in Houston, and Midway in Chicago, he notes. These smaller airports are generally closer to downtown, making it more convenient for business travelers and resulting in fewer delays than their same-city competitors.

In addition, the airline worked to create a corporate culture that rewarded innovation and differentiation and spoke to emotion-based values. As part of the Southwest core value set, employees are encouraged to have fun, show individuality, and have an ownership stake in the airline (through profit sharing). The customer experience focuses on egalitarianism: flying is affordable, there's no first class, seats aren't assigned, and generally the earlier you check in the earlier you board.

Let's look specifically at US Airways and Southwest, using the three key branding elements of creating an emotional connection, being instantly recognizable, and humanizing the experience/being audience centric.

SOUTHWEST		
EMOTIONAL CONNECTION	**INSTANTLY RECOGNIZABLE**	**HUMANIZED EXPERIENCE**
Southwest Airlines takes a new approach to air travel, focusing on low fares, fun, and travel without restrictions. They've implemented no baggage fees and no change fees and let staff loosen up on their interactions with customers. As such, customers have become loyal to their brand.	Visually Southwest is different from US Airways and other airlines on many fronts: plane color, flight attendant uniforms, cabin seating, and even services offered. It would be easy to spot a Southwest plane on a runway.	Southwest has worked to be customer-centric. From the boarding process to the flight safety presentation, they include customers in the process and keep the experience different and light.
US AIRWAYS		
EMOTIONAL CONNECTION	**INSTANTLY RECOGNIZABLE**	**HUMANIZED EXPERIENCE**
US Airways, like most legacy airline carriers, has very little that differentiates them or allows for a personal connection. They charge baggage and change fees, run similar routes, and appear interchangeable with other legacy carriers.	There is a reason that it is difficult to accurately describe the logo for US Airways. They have worked to create homogenous plane colors, flight attendant uniforms, and cabins. It is hard to differentiate their services from those of other airlines.	Through airlines mergers and consolidations, it has become difficult for US Airways to customize a customer experience. This challenge can be seen with most of the legacy airlines and US Airways faces the same issue.

Let's close out the brand examples with the power of Starbucks—a company that has branded not just a coffee business but also drink sizes, drink names, and the ubiquitous green logo.

We Met at Starbucks

Meg and Hamilton Swan met at Starbucks.

They were characters in the mock documentary *Best in Show,* a parody (among other things) of competitive dog shows. In one of the movie's scenes they engage in a dialogue that speaks to brand power.

By the way, if you actually know what some of the drinks are in this dialogue, you've been "branded!"

Meg: We had met at Starbucks. Not at the same Starbucks, we saw each other at different Starbucks across the street from each other. And Hamilton got up the courage to walk across the street one day and approached me.

Hamilton: I'd seen you in law school before. And I know that sometimes I'd be in one Starbucks and you'd be in the other Starbucks and then I'd think maybe I should go over to that Starbucks the next weekend and then you'd be at the other Starbucks. I remember what I was drinking when I met you. It was a grande espresso.

Meg: That's right, and I thought that was really sexy.

Hamilton: Yeah.

Meg: I was drinking cappuccinos and then I went to lattes and now a double espresso macchiato.

Hamilton: And now I'm big old chai tea latte soymilk kind of guy . . . because of the lactose. And then I walked across the street and there you were. And oh my gosh.

Meg: Working on my Mac.

Hamilton: And I had my Mac. And then I look over and she is reading J. Crew. It's so weird because I was such a huge J. Crew person then too. Still am. We sometimes like to go to Starbucks on weekends and take an LL Bean catalog and I'll say 'honey, what's new?" And she has five minutes to look through it and find what's new.

Meg: They've been around forever. We are so lucky. We are so lucky to have been raised amongst catalogs . . .

Starbucks. J. Crew. Mac . . .
Not bad for a short dialogue.

What is it about Starbucks that makes us pay at least four bucks for pretty much everything they sell?

Why do we speak a new language of tall, grande, and venti when we simply want to order a small, medium, or large drink?

How have they created such a powerful brand, in fact, so powerful that the ubiquitous coffeehouse chain was deemed the "most loved" of 3,400 food and restaurant brands, according to an analysis of social media sentiment conducted by Digital CoCo, a marketing agency?

Starbucks created a customer-centric brand experience.

As the customer, you were at the front of the Starbucks model (custom drinks, your name on the cup). People developed emotional connections with both their drinks and even the baristas who were serving them.

In addition, Starbucks created what they called a "third place," a place between work and home that would foster a sense of community and conversation. Their mission, Starbucks claims, is to inspire and nurture the human spirit—"one person, one cup, and one neighborhood at a time."

As Nancy Koehn of the Harvard Business School notes, Starbucks broke all kinds of brand "rules" along their road to success. They refused to franchise, thus pouring profits back into an infrastructure of company-owned stores.

And they did very little advertising or direct marketing. Instead, they spent their marketing resources on their stores, their employees (who received health care benefits if they worked more than twenty hours a week), and the customer experience.

As Koehn points out, "By focusing on the customer experience in company-owned stores, Starbucks created widespread consumer engagement not only in what the company was offering—specialty coffee served as the customer specified—but in the actual creation and promotion of the brand itself. There are few better examples of the power of customer word-of-mouth in entrepreneurial brand building than Starbucks."

As time has passed, Starbucks has been effective at targeting key influencers and adapting to the social media world. Paul Barron, founder of DigitalCoCo, told NBC News that Starbucks offers Web specials for "Coffee Heroes" and apps for paying by smart phones.

"They are fostering a digital lifestyle that is extending the brand experience beyond their four walls," he said. Online mentions by key influencers who use Twitter, Instagram, Facebook, and other social media "have a lot of effect on a lot of people." These are people with not just large followings but engaged followers.

Starbucks has become a cultural symbol, pushed originally by word-of-mouth marketing and now through social media "word of mouth." The process online is the same as offline: targeting influencers, developing emotional connectivity, and then letting them market their product. It has become so successful that their more than 34 million Facebook fans are actively part of the brand's success and experience. Fans are asked for their feedback on products and rewarded, with free drinks or other products, for engagement with the brand. Starbucks has used this information for creating or modifying products and offerings as well as developing brand loyalty.

We can look at the three key elements of branding using Starbucks as the model.

EMOTIONAL CONNECTION	INSTANTLY RECOGNIZABLE	HUMANIZED EXPERIENCE
Christine Nagy, who works in Silicon Valley, shows the brand connection in a quote she provided the *Wall Street Journal*. "For me, it's a daily necessity or I start getting withdrawals." Her standard order was a custom drink: a decaf grande nonfat no-whip no-foam extra-cocoa mocha; when the baristas saw her come through the door, Christine told the WSJ reporter, "They just [said,] 'We need a Christine here.'"	Starbucks, and the green-and-white twin-tailed mermaid, are easy to spot. Of course, it doesn't hurt that Starbucks is now in nearly every city I've ever traveled to. They developed a logo that connects with their company philosophy and even planted stores in high-visibility locations.	Starbucks places the customer at the center of the experience. When I was growing up, coffee was either regular or decaf (leaded or unleaded). The only customization was cream and sugar. Now the entire coffee "experience" is in the hands of the customer and Starbucks has globalized that concept. In addition, they've sought to create a "third place" between work and home—a community space.

The strength of the brand has helped inoculate Starbucks against some of the arguments that they were pushing out mom-and-pop coffee shops, hurting coffee farmers, and even attempting to "Americanize" other areas through their international expansion.

In fact, as John Simons, author of a book on Starbucks' success, noted that Starbucks leader Howard Schultz has expressed that the company is genuinely interested in cultures beyond the U.S. As a branding tactic, Starbucks openly displays its beans from "exotic locations—Sumatra, Kenya, Guatemala, Costa Rica, Ethiopia" to speak "for an awareness of a wider world." Something that Schultz calls "romancing the bean."

Debbie Millman, author of *Brand Thinking, and Other Noble Pursuits,* points out that "there are a few brands that have been elevated by their loyal advocates to actual tribes—the most exalted of groups—Apple, Nike for example—and more recently—Starbucks."

Starbucks is a cultural symbol, something for the cool crowd, that continues to strengthen their brand. Fashionistas and movie stars will never be seen carrying a Big Mac, but give them a decaf grande nonfat no-whip no-foam extra-cocoa mocha and expect to see some posing for the paparazzi.

Now Go Do It

There are some simple steps you need to follow to successfully create your brand.

The first thing to remember is that successful brands stem from successful narratives. A candidate with a great logo and tagline but with an established narrative of untrustworthiness won't end up possessing a strong brand. Or the brand of that individual won't exactly be something he or she would like.

Assuming you have developed a strong narrative, here are some things to keep in mind.

First, what is a brand?

> ➤ A named product or service, such as Toyota, Ivory Soap, or the BBC News. This refers to the branded product or service.

➤ A trademark such as Panasonic or Target, referring to the
    name or symbol
➤ A customer's beliefs about a product or service

As we saw with Apple and Hair Club for Men, a customer's belief
and connection is the most important element of a brand.

So how do you build a strong brand?

Step One: Build an emotional connection.

Step Two: Develop an instantly recognizable logo, image, or tagline.

Step Three: Create a humanizing of the experience, allowing the
audience to be a part of the brand.

Ask yourself whether your brand answers the following questions
in these three categories:

EMOTIONAL CONNECTION	INSTANTLY RECOGNIZABLE	HUMANIZED EXPERIENCE
Does the brand we are creating connect with people? Does it speak to them with more than just facts and figures?	Are my brand logo and tagline relevant to my narrative and messaging? Do they hold their own and reflect my product without additional explanation? Is my product, or am I (if an individual brand), visible to my audience?	Is my audience a participant in my brand's experience? Are real people depicted in my stories? Can people envision that my product is for people "just like me"?

If you are building your brand off of a strong narrative and can
offer something with an emotional connection, a recognizable and an
authentic (humanizing) experience, you will have the elements of a
strong brand.

CHAPTER 5

IMAGES

What About the Picture? Going Beyond Facts

What if you had developed a food product that was a reflection of good health: an all-natural mixture of whole grains that is fortified with vitamins? Imagine you had this product widely available, at an accessible price, during the beginning of the modern health food craze.

Sounds like a slam-dunk, right?

Well, for General Mills it wasn't quite that simple. In the late 1970s General Mills was riding high with Total cereal.

You know, the blue box that you try to avoid eye contact with when you are buying your frosted-covered sugar bombs?

But by the early 1980s Total was losing market share. In fact, it had lost a significant amount of market share to its pesky health-nut cousin, granola. So General Mills execs commissioned a consumer image study to assess why granola was the choice of gorgeous people everywhere.

They found that 64 percent of granola consumers believed granola was much more nutritious than cereals like Total. In fact, most people surveyed didn't even know that Total was a fortified cereal.

The execs knew they needed to reach out to this demographic, especially to women, who made up a disproportionate share of the cereal-buying public.

How would they do it?

Well, they had numbers on their side; after all theirs was the only 100 percent fortified cereal. And so they tested two fact-based commercials with focus groups. These test commercials showed the side of the box with uninspiring and unmoving images like Vitamin A = 100% and Vitamin D = 100%.

Neither of the commercials moved the needle.

But option three's commercial did.

For option three, the Madison Avenue advertising team came up with a catchy title: "bowl."

"Bowl" used images to convey, much more effectively, what numbers and facts couldn't.

The ad team set the stage with a stark table-top setting and two white bowls. The announcer poured a small serving of Total into the bowl and pointed out that it contained 100% of your daily vitamins and minerals. He then picked up a competing brand of granola and began to pour the amount needed to get the same nutritional level.

The granola bowl overflowed and spilled onto the table.

In twenty seconds General Mills was able to brand Total as *the* health cereal. And even today General Mills is still using ads for Total with minor variations of that visual.

The images were more powerful than simply stating the facts.

Images and the V-J Day Kiss

Images have the power to communicate what words and numbers can't. Television images of natural disasters like Hurricane Katrina and the earthquake and tsunami in Japan catalyzed people to give millions of dollars in donations to the Red Cross.

The images gave an emotional context to the numbers; a face to the words in the media.

Images also have the ability to put life into context and give meaning to facts. Think about two of the most powerful images of World War II.

More than 25,000 people were killed or injured during the Battle of Iwo Jima, but nothing brought the reality of those numbers home more than the picture of six heroes raising the flag on Mount Suribachi. And nothing brought the joy of the war's end like the photo of the V-J Day kiss in Times Square.

These images have endured for generations even as the numbers associated with the war have faded.

Why is this?

It turns out we're wired to understand images better than words. And we even put words *into images* to help us remember the words.

Cheryl Grady co-authored a paper for the National Institutes of Sciences revealing that the human brain overwhelmingly remembers images better than words.

Or, as she explained it, the study "examined the neural correlates of memory for pictures and words in the context of episodic memory encoding to determine material-specific differences in brain activity patterns."

That summary proved they didn't follow their own thesis! Try remembering that in thirty seconds.

The paper noted that people are able to remember more than 2,000 pictures with at least 90 percent accuracy in recognition tests. This recollection can occur even if subjects are exposed to the images over a short period of time.

One theory, advanced by psychologist Allan Paivio, that pictures engage associations and knowledge an individual has about the world. Pictures can complement the words and vice-versa.

Paivio's dual-coding theory (fancy scientist name) argues that visual and verbal information are processed differently.

For example, you can think of a car visually or think of the textual word "car." But which has more staying power?

The image.

Verbal information is enhanced when you can create a relevant visual.

For some reason this doesn't stop your co-worker from giving you a text-laden death by PowerPoint presentation.

Do you remember a presentation's sales numbers? Or do you remember the simple sales graph that depicts the same information?

It's important to communicate visually with your audience. People need to be able to see and feel your words or the words will fall flat.

Facts are just facts without image and emotion. This is something that advertisers, such as the makers of the "bowl" ad, have understood for quite some time.

Research by cognitive scientists, especially recent research because of the improvement of magnetic resonance imaging (MRI), has shown how our brains engage with information better when presented with visuals and text.

This "multiple representation principle," as coined by Dr. Richard E. Mayer, explains how using two modes of representation (visual and textual) works better than simply using text alone.

For example, Dr. Mayer notes that "students who listened to a narration explaining how a bicycle tire pump works while also viewing a corresponding animation generated twice as many useful solutions to subsequent problem-solving transfer questions than did students who listened to the same narration without viewing any animation."

Research in cognitive theory has shown that creating emotionally compelling combinations of text and visuals, as opposed to relying on text alone, "allows for the person to build two different mental representations—a verbal model and a visual model—and build connections between them."

You need to engage your audience in multiple ways and visuals are an essential element to that equation.

The Tale of Barbara Tarbox

In 2002, when Barbara Tarbox was diagnosed with stage-four lung cancer at the age of forty-one, she had been smoking since she was eleven years old.

As the Canadian Broadcast Company told it, "She took the diagnosis as a call to arms: she travelled to schools across Canada and spoke to the media, using her own cancer-wracked body to tell of the dangers of smoking."

But what made Barbara so powerful wasn't that she laid out a Surgeon's General Warning speech. You know the type: "Smoking Is Bad For Your Health." Not exactly something that will convince people of anything.

No, instead Barbara used images to connect emotionally with the people she spoke with. She would often describe her pain in graphic terms.

"Look at my arms," she told one group of Edmonton children just months after being diagnosed with cancer. "I don't know if you can see it but it's where the bones stick out. And you know what happens? When your tissues start to die, they turn black. Oh yes, people. They turn black. And there isn't a perfume on the market that can hide that smell. All the result of smoking."

She didn't try the lackluster governmental campaigns that use facts or numbers about cancer; she used images of herself to convince people to not smoke.

And these images were so powerful that ten years later her family is trying to use her likeness, specifically a hospital bed picture taken of her in the last days of her life, as the lead photo in an antismoking campaign in Canada and the United States.

Focus groups of smokers in Canada have rated these deathbed images as having the greatest impact of the proposed antismoking campaigns.

In the U.S. the Food and Drug Administration (FDA) is looking at a set of nine required warnings for cigarette packs, each of which has one color graphic and one of the nine textual warning statements. The antiquated Surgeon's General Warning is getting a much-needed update.

One of those images is a picture of Barbara Tarbox covering one side of the pack with the words "WARNING: Cigarettes Cause Cancer."

The FDA administrator said the usage of images marked a "crucial step toward reducing the tremendous toll of illness and death caused by tobacco. The health consequences of smoking will be obvious every time someone picks up a pack of cigarettes."

No longer will the small side of a pack of cigarettes have a few words that don't resonate.

Lawyers and Underwater Basket Weaving

In 1963, Harold Weiss and J. B. McGrath, Jr. published a seminal book on the relationship between visuals and retention. They wrote it for the audience most unable to communicate clearly: engineers and scientists. But more recently their study was shown to help another hopeless group: lawyers.

We'll get to the lawyers in a minute.

According to Weiss and McGrath, people retain information at differing levels depending on how it is presented.

That makes sense. You retain nothing in your fourth-century Greek literature class but everything in your underwater basket weaving class. But why?

For starters, there aren't a lot of words or facts in underwater basket weaving. And Weiss and McGrath show that words and facts alone are difficult for an individual to retain.

The Weiss and McGrath study shows that after three days an individual retains 10 percent of information after it has been presented only verbally (score one for basket weaving retention). Weiss and McGrath note that retention rates increase to 20 percent when people are given only visual information. And that number explodes to 65 percent if it is a combination of words and images.

Successful lawyers have started to catch on to this. But they have faced an interesting disconnect that many in the business and political worlds face: you teach similarly to how you learn.

This rule is well documented. If you are an auditory learner, as the majority of lawyers are, you will try to sway others with words. If you're a visual learner, as the majority of the rest of society are, you will use images, too.

So knowing this, you need to be willing to break out of your learning comfort zone to reach your audience.

No longer can the trial lawyer rely on the Matlock closing argument. In fact, lawyers are starting to use visuals or emotionally charged images with their arguments in order to sway juries.

Advertisers and politicians with their campaigns, or anyone who is attempting to sway public opinion, need to reach audiences in the way their audiences learn best.

The Weiss and McGrath study backs up this technique. Measuring retention rates at various timed intervals, they found large drop-offs when audiences were given only verbal information. For example, their study found that people retained at least 70 percent of information, regardless of presentation, for the first three hours. After seventy-two hours, however, these numbers dropped exponentially to the 10, 20, and 65 percent retention rates listed above.

Why would this matter?

For starters, it doesn't do you much good to be selling something that people can't remember the next day. Or if you're a lawyer, you want jurors to remember your compelling argument long into the deliberations process. And if you're in politics, you want a voter to remember you well after your TV interview is over.

So how do you do this?

You can start by thinking like a kindergarten teacher.

A is for Apple

Think back to the question I posed at the beginning of this book: Why do college professors unsuccessfully communicate with statistics and facts while kindergarten teachers captivate through stories and pictures?

As an American History major in college I made it pretty far before I realized I needed to fulfill some science credits. Like any good student of humanities I looked for something with minimal math and found my calling in astronomy. After all, I was pretty good with a telescope so I figured I would have this class down pat.

But telescopes, nebulas, and red stars weren't commonplace in that class.

Why not?

My professor found comfort in the overhead projector.

For those under a certain age an overhead projector consists of three things that ensures it will be a failure at visual communications: a bright lamp connected to a large square (gray) box, a fan to cool it, and transparent sheets that the professor could write or show text on, which was projected onto a large screen.

And this is just what my professor did. Mathematical equations, written and displayed on an overhead projector, were cross-referenced to preprinted outlines. It was the early version of death by Power-Point without the speed of clicking through slides.

This was astronomy. Just think about the visual possibilities!

Now think about an overhead projector as the only source of visuals.

Needless to say, it wasn't my top grade in college. But one of the things it helped illustrate is how we communicate subjects.

The reason I was excited to take astronomy (other than fulfilling a science credit) was to see the visuals. There is no doubt it is a complex subject, but it's one that is visually based. Without the visuals, however, the math had no meaning or context. And without the visuals, it was hard to sustain interest.

If only college professors would remember back to kindergarten.

Recently I went back to my elementary school in San Diego. My kindergarten classroom looked the same—except the chairs looked significantly smaller.

Just like my niece's kindergarten classroom, the room was visually oriented: the walls were decorated with images to teach words; desks had pictures of letters corresponding to pictures; animals and shapes were scattered about with sounds and colors described below.

In my former classroom stood one of the most common visuals in a kindergarten classroom: the alphabet, encircling the room from A to Z with corresponding images next to each letter.

A is for Apple.

B is for Ball.

Learning the alphabet is a key early educational attainment. Before entering kindergarten most kids have learned the ABCs song. The song is sung to the same tune of "Twinkle Twinkle Little Star," but unlike that song and most other songs, no images are conjured up while singing it.

As Dr. Paul Martin Lester points out in a paper on visual communications, with "Twinkle, we can look up in the night's sky and imagine a little star out of the billions shining just for us. But a song about the letters in the alphabet does not carry any visual equivalents."

So how do kids make the transition from letters to meaning?

Dr. Lester Martin notes that children are taught to connect concrete nouns with images for each letter in the song—like A is for Apple.

"Each letter of the alphabet becomes a picture that corresponds with a complex set of direct and mediated images. We no longer have to think of an actual red, juicy apple. We can simply see the letter 'A' and know that it stands for that fruit."

Just as we do with our ABCs, we are taught early on to connect words and images, to learn through visuals. This is why nearly everything that kindergarten teachers do is through visual connections.

Clearly it works.

The concepts of language are as new to a child as the mathematical theories of astronomy are to a college student. Yet they are often taught in different ways, and if my grade in astronomy were any indication, with differing success levels.

Boring—But Quality

Over the last forty years the share of import vehicle sales in the U.S. has exploded. But in the fall of 1977, marketing execs at Audi were trying to figure out how they could boost their sluggish sales by tapping into the U.S. market.

At the time, Audi was an unknown brand in the U.S. Volkswagen, their parent company, was mostly known for creating what president Heinz Nordhoff called a car with "the highest technical excellence at the lowest price."

Translation: boring but high-quality, cheap cars.

Audi knew they could offer cars to the U.S. market that were better engineered, more innovative, and more feature-laden than higher-priced luxury vehicles.

But how do you sell that?

Marketing execs took a novel approach to their ad campaign. As opposed to doing what all car companies do (glamour shots of a car driving down roads you will never drive down with families—roads that don't look real), they took a personal approach.

They used a simple and powerful image: a real person.

Known as the "engineering" ad by the sales team, the commercial told the story from the perspective of an engineer who actually designed the car. The engineer showed the style, lines, headroom, and power of the car, acting as the narrator the whole time. As Stephen Greyser noted in his integral book on advertising, the Audi ads were personal in tone with an engineer communicating directly to the consumer. "Aspects of 'craftsmanship' and 'German engineering' [received] prominence."

Sales jumped tenfold over the next eight years.

Audi didn't try to sell people on the facts of better engineering. They showed it with a simple visual.

Turns Out We Consume Too Much Salt

The Division for Heart Disease and Stroke Prevention at the Centers for Disease Control and Prevention (CDC) has a problem that is bigger than the length of their name.

Salt.

Apparently we love our salt, and scientists have had some trouble communicating to us the dangers of excessive sodium intake. Given that they're scientists and that they like studies, I would suggest they read the Weiss and McGrath study.

But the CDC had a better idea: Provide training on how to translate data into images.

The training was put on by Rachel Barron-Simpson, a health *scientist* at the CDC. She claims that data were often presented simply in their raw form or in a format that was not easily understood by an audience.

Take for example this article that appeared in the *New England Journal of Medicine*. Barron-Simpson notes that it appears the author wanted to convey a message about how sodium and diet relate to blood pressure.

Reducing the sodium intake from the high to the intermediate level reduced the systolic blood pressure by 2.1 mm Hg ($P<0.001$) during the control diet and by 1.3 mm Hg ($P=0.03$) during the DASH diet. Reducing the sodium intake from the intermediate to the low level caused additional reductions of 4.6 mm Hg during the control diet (P<0.001) and 1.7 mm Hg during the DASH diet (P<0.01). The effects of sodium were observed in participants with and in those without hypertension.

Based on this information, the audience may not have been able to glean the article's meaning at first glance. Most of us might not have been able to glean it after multiple glances.

So how do you translate information about systolic blood pressure and high salt diets into something that you could explain to the guy sitting next to you on a train?

Through a simple visual.

Limit the text to say what you really want to convey. In this case, "eating less salt could save your life." And back it up with a compelling, yet simple, visual that shows the relationship between salt and blood pressure.

Rosie the Riveter

Next to the images of the V-J Day kiss or the Iwo Jima flag raising, Rosie the Riveter's "We Can Do It" poster is one of the most enduring images of the Second World War.

Most can visualize the poster, created by J. Howard Miller for the Westinghouse War Production Committee, and immediately determine what that image was trying to convey.

Strength. Determination. Patriotism.

Rosie was saying that women working in nontraditional labor force positions had these three attributes.

That's a lot to convey with a simple image and a few words. But why was the image even created? After all, everyone knew that men were enlisting in large number to fight in the war so clearly there would be a labor shortage that women would need to fill.

Why not just put out a plea for help?

Well, it turns out the government tried that through a propaganda campaign. But the results were less than impressive.

So the government worked actively to shape wartime opinion, and to galvanize a new section of the labor force, through images.

Instead of creating a taskforce, the go-to solution when you don't have a solution, they created the Office of War Information. This aptly named governmental agency became part of the newly formed Advertising Council, a nonprofit, private working group of advertising execs that worked in concert with the government.

That's right. Professional advertising executives joined with the government to create images that persuade.

As Tawnya Adkins Covert notes in her book on wartime advertising, "The Ad Council played a primary role in the production of war-related images and messages for the United States government."

Loose Lips Sink Ships?

Check.

Rosie the Riveter.

Check.

These powerful images and short, catchy phrases created emotional connections with the country and had marked impacts. Women in the labor force increased nearly 50 percent during wartime and these wartime images were placed in magazines that targeted women.

The Advertising Council still exists today, creating iconic images like Smokey the Bear, the Crash Test Dummies, and McGruff the Crime Dog.

It's a prime example of telling stories and motivating actions through images as opposed to data.

Super Bowl!

I love sports.

Growing up in San Diego, the land of eternal sunshine, I spent more time outside than in. My brothers and I would play wiffleball in the backyard and football in the street. We grew up worshiping teams that no matter how much we tried to will them to victory would invariably depress us in either September/October (baseball season) or January/February (football season).

As sports groupies we're what the corporate world likes to call "consumers." After all, it turns out we're not the only ones who love sports . . . so do advertisers.

And consumers are best reached through powerful images.

Think about it. What is the ultimate proof of the power of imagery? How about spending nearly $4 million dollars for thirty seconds of images? If you were going to drop $4 million dollars on anything you'd better be sure it works. And companies across America do exactly that each year during the Super Bowl.

Why is it that they believe these thirty seconds, and the 100 million viewers it reaches, are worth the cost?

Why not buy more newspaper ads?

Sorry, newspaper advertising. Even though I still read you loyally everyday people just aren't that excited by a full-page national ad . . . even at one-twentieth the cost to the advertiser.

It's all about the image.

In fact, the ads are actually drawing people in to watch the Super Bowl. According to Bernice Kanner, who wrote a book on Super Bowl advertising, more than two out of three viewers pay attention to the commercials and more than half talk about them the next day. To top it off, about 10 percent of the people watch the game *just* for the ads.

Madison Avenue advertising agencies are willing to gamble $4 million for 30 seconds of images because they've found it isn't that much of a gamble.

Take Anheuser-Busch for example. Anheuser-Busch has spent millions on Super Bowl ads bringing us Spuds MacKenzie, the English bull terrier that became a cult figure as the Original Party Animal, the frogs that croaked "Bud-Weis-Errrr," and, most recently, Hank the Clydesdale horse.

These image-based advertising campaigns conveyed a sense of cool that text alone couldn't. In fact, with each ad Anheuser-Busch saw growth in sales between 17–19 percent during the month after the Super Bowl ad ran.

Other companies have had similar success. Apple's famous "1984" ad, Snickers "Betty White" ad, and General Motors' "Sad Robot" spot all received millions of dollars in free advertising as they were replayed by the media and continue to be watched virally.

All of these ads have something in common. As former worldwide advertising network exec Ted Sann said, "You need to show, more than tell, a story." His former worldwide advertising company, BBDO, recognized the power of images and this medium to reach an audience. BBDO "has a formula: tickle the funny bone, tug at the heartstrings and toss in a surprise ending," he explained.

In thirty seconds, using the power of images, the Super Bowl ads' companies created an emotionally compelling narrative. The result?

BBDO finds the ads so successful that they run multiple spots in each Super Bowl. So many, in fact that the Super Bowl has been nicknamed the "BBDO Bowl" in some advertising circles.

The Beasties and Shakespeare

If you're like me and 22 million other people in the U.S., you own a Beastie Boys record. The Beasties are the masters of hip hop; the ultimate party band.

In the mid 1980s their music ushered in a new era of commercial viability for rap music, breaking a significant glass ceiling for the genre. In fact, their 1986 album *License to Ill* (described as "three idiots create a masterpiece" by *Rolling Stone*) was the first rap album to reach #1 on the Billboard charts.

Their monster musical hooks notwithstanding, how do these "three idiots" create a memorable song?

More important, how do they write songs that you can remember?

With imagery.

Take the Grammy-winning song "Intergalactic."

At about 400 words it's nearly four times the length of the Beatles megahit "Yesterday"—and that's if you count the Mmm, mmm's!"

But "Intergalactic" has enjoyed massive commercial success. It's become a sing-along classic at beer-filled karaoke bars.

Here are some lyrics:

> *From the family tree of old school hip hop*
> *Kick off your shoes and relax your socks*
> *The rhymes will spread just like a pox*
> *Cause the music is live like an electric shock*

Think about the images this conjures. "Family tree . . . relax your socks . . . like a pox . . . electric shock." Just reading this once your head starts to nod and your mind begins to see the lyrics. With their imagery you can feel the rhythm and internalize the sense of the song.

Of course, they could have done the professorial version of the song:

> *From the historic lineage of hip hop*
> *Remove your shoes and please take off your socks*
> *The musical rhymes will be easily remembered*
> *Because the music is energetic and exciting*

Sound familiar? Seems like a typical boardroom presentation.

Without the imagery the lyrics fall flat. I guarantee you won't remember 400 words without those images.

I know you weren't expecting a Beastie Boys reference in this book; you are more learned than that. So how about some Shakespeare?

Back when I was trying to impress people I used to read Shakespeare aloud. In the eighth grade I even took a lead role in *Macbeth*. I remember going to the local college to rent some clothes for my part. I looked absolutely ridiculous.

Just a couple of years later (just a couple), I still remember some of my lines.

Think about it. Even you know some of his lines.

Why?

In part because Shakespeare is the man with a plan when it comes to imagery. Like this from Act V of *Macbeth*:

> *"Out out, brief candle! Life's but a walking shadow, a poor player that struts and frets his hour upon the stage and then is heard no more: it is a tale told by an idiot, full of sound and fury, signifying nothing."*

Okay, no one said he was uplifting. But he does draw a nice mental picture for you. It's largely why he has been able to make eighth graders recite his lines 400 years after his death.

Remember, we are wired to remember images. When we want to remember text we even put it into images. Why not simplify your audiences' lives and do it for them?

Now Go Do It

We are built to understand images better than we understand words. And we even put words *into images* to help us remember the words. Verbal information is enhanced when you can create a relevant visual—even if that visual is simply a mental picture your audience creates.

But how do you best integrate visuals?

Here are three easy steps:

1. **Use imagery with your words**—create a mental picture for your audience
2. **Use actual images**—incorporate the pictures that would represent the words you are trying to convey
3. **Connect emotion to images**—if the visual (mental or actual) has emotional connection it will resonate

Here is a simple matrix to help you integrate visuals, or words that evoke mental pictures, more easily.

IMAGERY WITH WORDS	USING IMAGES ONLY	EMOTIONAL CONNECTION
1. If you don't have an actual visual does the language you present create a mental picture? 2. Think back to the Beastie Boys and Shakespeare—does your language choice draw a mental picture for your audience?	1. Images are remembered more than words. Can you use an image to show what you are trying to say? 2. Think back to Rosie the Riveter. Take the key points you are trying to convey and attempt to find an image that will complement those points.	1. Pictures are just pictures without emotional connection. During wartime Rosie the Riveter connected emotionally on many different levels. 2. When choosing an image ask, "Does this image represent my message? Does it emotionally connect?"

CHAPTER 6

FRAMING

Death and Taxes Are Still Certain

It turns out that dead people hate to be taxed.

I've haven't heard that firsthand, but according to some polling on the term "death tax" it seems to be the case.

But what exactly it is about a "death tax" that people find so unappealing? Other than, you know, the obvious?

The answer may lie in how the term came about and how people sometimes "frame" issues to their advantage.

So before we look at taxing people who are six feet under let's look at what the term "framing" means.

Framing is one of the most widely used buzz terms in political science, psychology, communications studies, and, more recently, business. Public relations people, politicians, and other professions that start with a "p" think framing is the answer to every problem.

But what exactly is it?

Robert Entman, a professor at George Washington University who has written extensively on framing, argues that the term is defined as "any effort to influence public opinion through the formulation of messages."

This makes sense.

After all, the point of framing a message a certain way is to present it in the best possible light for your situation.

Why? To influence public opinion.

But there is an even simpler definition courtesy of Shanto Iyengar, a communications professor at Stanford: presenting the same information in different ways.

While there are probably smart people holding smart people conferences that are debating this term's definition as you read, I vote for the simple definition.

How does simply presenting something in a different way influence public opinion?

Let's look back at taxing the dead to see just how frames are used.

The death tax, also known as the inheritance tax or estate tax, applies to less than 2 percent of Americans. According to the IRS, it is a tax imposed on transferable property of a deceased person including cash and securities, real estate, insurance, trusts, annuities, business interests, and other assets that exceed the exclusion amount (which has ranged from $1,500,000 in 2004 to $5,250,000 in 2013).

Because it applies to fewer than 1 in 50 people it is the kind of thing that many people didn't know or care about, until a political framing debate took place in the mid to late 1990s.

In the mid 1990s the term began to catch on among conservative political leaders, including House Speaker Newt Gingrich, hoping to draw attention to this tax they wanted eliminated.

It's great that a small group of political leaders want something eliminated. But how do you get the average person to care about something that doesn't apply to him? Even more important, how do you get him to care about something that has the name "estate tax" or "inheritance tax," which implies that it not only *doesn't* apply to him but *only* applies to people who have cool things like estates?

So the Republican leadership encouraged their colleagues to use the term "death tax" instead to make the public think the tax applied to more people than it actually did.

In other words, they sought to reframe the debate on the tax in a new way.

And according to research done by political science professors Brian Schaffner and Mary Layton Atkinson, the phrase "death tax" became a common term in a short time. Initially, it showed up in media accounts just 11 times between 1989 and 1996 while "estate tax" was used 454 times during the same period. By the late 1990s, however, both terms were being used relatively equally.

But why would it matter if you called something by a new name?

Let's look at the two possible frames: estate tax and death tax.

In this case, you could either frame it as an "estate tax"—a label that Brian Schaffner notes would draw attention to the assumedly wealthy families "privileged enough to own estates." This term would convey that most Americans would not have to pay the tax.

Many Democrats at the time, and still today, use the term "estate tax" to highlight that it only applies to small group of people.

Or, you could call it a "death tax" to highlight that the tax was unfair. And since everyone dies, you can assume it applies to you in some way.

Which do you think has more emotional resonance? Are you telling me the government wants to tax you while you're alive *and* dead? Seems a bit unfair.

Since fairness is an important value for many of us, Schaffner notes, "an appeal on these terms might be persuasive to an individual even if that individual would not be subject to the tax."

"Death tax" had an emotional connection to the targeted audience. Since Republican leaders wanted to build awareness and support for their stance on the issue, even though it didn't apply to much of their audience, they knew that by simply using this newly framed phrase many would think that the tax *could apply to anyone—even me*.

This was the ultimate frame. Presenting the same information in different ways; specifically, in a way that benefits your cause.

But the question is did the framing work?

In many ways the answer is yes. By the late 1990s and into the 2000 presidential election, the Republicans employed a coordinated strategy to repeal the inheritance tax. Nearly every political speech and talking point featured the term "death tax."

In 2000, Nicholas Lemann wrote an article for *The New Yorker* that took a behind-the-scenes look at why certain terms were used in political campaigns and how focus groups were used. More specifically, Lemann was looking at the framing of the presidential election and how certain issues become relevant during a campaign.

In part, he looked at a focus group conducted by Frank Luntz, a well-known Republican political consultant and wordsmith. The group's topic? The death tax.

As Luntz conducted the focus group, he asked people what they would most want to eliminate: an estate tax, an inheritance tax, or a death tax. As you can imagine, death tax was number one on the list.

In fact, Lemann noted, the focus group "vented for a while about how deeply unfair it was that you work hard your whole life and the government taxes it all away in the end."

Never mind that the tax didn't apply to anyone in the room. Luntz knew that by getting the term injected into the political debate the pendulum of public opinion would swing more toward the Republican Party on this issue.

And it did.

As a result of this framing more people believed the tax would apply to them than it actually would. It also placed the issue front and center in the legislative and media debates, making a large issue out of something that didn't affect the majority of people.

Because of work by Luntz and other Republican political leaders, the media, political talking heads, and soon the average voter began using the newly framed term. This frame greatly increased the consciousness of the issue to the average taxpayer and ultimately had an impact on the legislative debate. Within a few short years a tax that simply wasn't on the radar of most people became part of the regular lexicon.

In fact, it even led to legislative changes on the inheritance tax— the goal of the proponents of the "death tax" debate.

According to Mayling Birney, who studied public opinion on the issue while a postdoctoral fellow at Princeton University, the policy action taken on the tax was not a true reflection of public opinion but rather a generated opinion based on the framing.

"Surveys consistently show that the number of people in favor of repeal [of the tax] drops when respondents are given information on . . . how many people pay," she found.

Why exactly did the term "death tax" work?

It's important to note that simply using a different term or framing something in a new way *isn't* what leads to success. Just like messaging and branding, for framing to be effective in influencing perception it needs to play into a strong and established narrative *and* have an emotional connection.

After all, Republicans have been working on a narrative of "smaller government and less taxes" since the Reagan Revolution. Therefore it made sense to reframe a tax issue. It played into an established narrative a few decades in the making.

So what are the keys of a successful frame?

➤ Emotional Impact
➤ Relevance and Ease of Understanding
➤ Conflict (does it create two clear sides and provide contrast?)

We will examine these elements more in depth in a second, but first let's consider the threshold question for a successful frame: does the framing apply to an underlying narrative? The answer is yes, as tax issues have been a feature of the Republican narrative for a few decades.

Now let's look at the three key components in the context of the death tax:

EMOTIONAL IMPACT	RELEVANT/ UNDERSTANABLE	CONFLICT
Death tax has a strong emotional component. It simply doesn't seem fair that you can be taxed during life *and* death. So the term had resonance and played into fears that even if you worked hard and played by the rules all of it could be taken away at the end.	This was a key component to the success of the frame. An "estate tax" was simply not relevant to 99% of the population but a "death tax" appeared relevant to 100% of the population. The applicability didn't change but the new term made people think it did.	An estate tax is something that applies to "them." But a death tax applies to "me." Anytime you have things that apply to "me" you've introduced the conflict and now have two clear sides: the government and me (as opposed to the government, "them," and "me").

If you have a frame that hits on these three elements it is more likely to stick. Now let's take a closer look at how to construct a successful frame.

Elements of a Successful Frame

Let's say taxing dead people isn't your thing. Maybe you have a business and you're trying to figure out the best way to showcase your core message.

It might sound elementary, but one of the key steps to take is to understand who your audience is. Scott Cutlip, author of *Effective Public Relations,* put it this way: your audience consists of people— these people live, work, worship, and play in the framework of social institutions in cities, suburbs, et cetera.

Each person is subject to many influences of which the communicator's message is typically only one small source of influence. People tend to read, watch, or listen to communications that present points of view with which they are sympathetic or in which they have a personal stake (think Fox News or MSNBC).

So you need to understand the backgrounds, beliefs, and behaviors of the people involved that you're trying to reach. Then you need to focus on *how* they are being reached. Otherwise, framing a message won't have much impact if you don't understand how to get the message to land effectively with the end user.

In the case of the death tax, a number of political leaders first reached out to sympathetic conservative publications. These publications started using the term and framing the issue in a way that reflected what the political leaders wanted. The audience that read these targeted publications were receptive to the message and helped push the message to more mainstream outlets.

The result? The term was used in the mainstream media and the ultimate target, the average voter, was reached.

Think about it. When was the last time you watched the cooking channel and saw an ad for men's underwear? How about what you see while watching a playoff sports game? Car, beer, and pizza ads?

This is knowing your audience.

In messaging campaigns, such as advertising for your business, effective frames reflect a strong understanding of differing communities.

As the TV ads above suggest, the advent of specialized media allows you to reach targeted audiences with a targeted message and frame. Want to take out an ad about the death tax? I wouldn't suggest running it on the Cartoon Network on a Saturday morning. But how about that same ad at 9:00 P.M. on Fox News?

So let's look again at the keys of a successful frame by taking each component individually. We'll revisit the yogurt commercial example that we explored in the chapter on narrative.

> ➤ Emotional Impact
> ➤ Relevance and Ease of Understanding
> ➤ Conflict (does it create two clear sides and provide contrast?)

Emotional Impact: Everyone has thought about their appearance at some point in their lives. And few things can have a stronger emotional impact than how you look or feel about yourself. That is why so much money is spent on health and fitness. The yogurt ad has an emotional impact: unsure if you'll fit into that bathing suit in time for summer? We can fix it—just eat our product. The yogurt company could have framed their message in a number of ways: We have a lot of exciting active cultures! We just released five new flavors that try to emulate something that tastes good! Both of those things are true, but they don't have an emotional impact. By framing yogurt as a weight management tool, the yogurt brand says a lot in thirty seconds and creates a powerful message.

Relevance and Ease of Understanding: Effective frames must be designed for the situation (context) and audience. They are often used by audiences to make sense of issues or to simplify something complex. As Professor Matthew Nisbet writes, frames enable your audience to understand a complex topic with greater relevance to their lives. In other words, a successful frame will communicate why an issue matters to your audience in a simple way. Want to fit into the bathing suit? Eat our yogurt. It's not an accident that these ads are run in the spring just a few months before the summer bathing suit season, when it's most relevant.

Conflict [Two Clear Sides]: You may remember that one of the keys to a strong narrative is a struggle that is followed by some sort of resolution. For the yogurt commercial the struggle is overcoming chocolate cravings and your friend's peer pressure for pizza night, and the resolution is a Hawaiian dream vacation with a perfectly fitting bathing suit. All because you eat their yogurt. Framing is similar. Successful frames have two clear sides—in this case, pizza versus a bathing suit that fits—and the conflict is inherent in this scenario. The yogurt company is framing their message to say that by simply eating their product you will be in Hawaii looking great.

Connection to Narrative: This last element isn't a component of constructing a frame but without it the frame will not succeed. A successful frame cannot simply be a rewording of something to your advantage. Many political leaders have tried to come up with terms that resonate but failed at creating an underlying narrative that let the frame work. Using the yogurt example again, yogurt manufacturers have been working for years to showcase their product as a health food. Through everything they have advertised and done they have established a simple narrative: if you eat yogurt, you will be healthy. Therefore it made sense for our yogurt brand to frame their yogurt as something that would help out with your summer look.

Successful frames stem from strong narratives. In order to construct your frame you should work off of a narrative foundation and strong core message. Without these elements your frame won't stick.

This is a key point. Even if you create a frame with an emotional connection, resonance, and contrast/conflict it will not stand without the underlying narrative.

Let's take a look at another example.

I'd Rather Recover than Stimulate

President Barack Obama didn't waste much time in trying to recover the economy after his 2008 election. In fact, four days after taking office he delivered his first radio address to the nation in which he spoke about the American Recovery and Reinvestment Act.

The "Recovery" Act.

But wasn't the Recovery Act the same thing as the "stimulus package"?

Yep.

But polling showed that voters didn't support a "stimulus package." In fact, according to a CNN poll at the time, 56 percent of respondents didn't like the idea of a stimulus.

But economic recovery?

The same poll found that about eight in ten people polled favored government spending on roads and bridges and aid for unemployed workers and soon-to-be-laid-off cops and teachers.

In other words, as Patrick Sellers, a political science professor at Davidson College who has written several books on framing, points out, "The public was more willing to support an economic *recovery* package than an economic *stimulus*." The public was even more supportive of the legislation when specifically told how the money would be spent.

So what did the president do?

In his first radio address to the nation, President Obama did not use the word stimulus once in his 806-word address. Instead, Sellers points out, he framed the legislation as needed "recovery," focusing almost entirely on the programs the spending would support.

It turns out there is a reason for using this type of framing beyond polling and focus groups. According to a pair of Stanford University business professors who looked at the marketing of the Recovery Act, people were much more likely to accept risky prospects when the prospects are presented in the context of avoiding losses (recovery) rather than achieving gains (stimulus).

This is known to social scientists as the "prospect theory."

Indeed, the professors found evidence for the strong impact of framing effects on public opinion: support for the stimulus varied substantially when it was framed as "preventing a collapse" in the economy as opposed to "boosting" the economy. The public preferred a recovery.

But even though there was a desire to call it "recovery," many, including the media and a number of Democrats supporting the bill, still continued to call it a stimulus. So why didn't the "recovery" frame take hold?

Did the Recovery Act frame fail to have emotional components, relevance, or two clear sides?

Let's deconstruct it a bit. First, we should look at the entire name: The American Recovery and Reinvestment Act (ARRA).

Let's be honest. Calling something the American Recovery and Reinvestment Act doesn't really have that "death tax" cachet. And this is problematic given that the term "stimulus," shown to be unpopular in multiple opinion polls, was already established. So to counter an established frame you need to have a viable counterframe.

ARRA didn't cut it.

But there was some hope with the term "recovery" and focusing on the "Recovery Act."

After all, there is emotional resonance in helping something heal and recover. Many were facing some of the worst economic times seen in their lives, and the need for preventing something from becoming even worse had a strong emotional connection.

And it had relevance in that people were feeling the strains of the economy at the time the bill was being proposed.

Was it understandable?

Yes and no. People could get that they needed a recovery—that we needed to prevent things from dropping even further. But it was hard to see how this "recovery" would relate to the individual.

Did it have two clear sides?

Yes.

So if most of the elements of a successful frame were met, why didn't the term take hold?

The main issue was with the underlying narrative.

The ARRA/Recovery/Stimulus was up against a strong narrative of simply being too expensive; therefore, the ultimate value was already in question.

ARRA was falling victim to what some in psychology call "anchoring," a term used to describe the common tendency to rely too heavily, or "anchor," on only one piece of information when making decisions.

In other words, a decision is based on one piece of information even if it isn't relevant. In investing, many people use stock prices as an anchor. For example, you may see a stock has dropped from $75 to $50 so you believe, based on the anchor that it was $75, that it is a good deal. However, there are many other components as to whether a stock is a good investment beyond the price.

In the case of the ARRA, researchers found there was a strong anchor—the cost of the bill—especially in association with other bailout packages that had recently passed.

Many were predisposed to believe the bill cost too much.

The result? A narrative being established that focused on the *cost* of the bill as opposed to the *results* that the bill was expected to create.

Until the narrative was solidified to focus on the potential results the frame would fall flat. It didn't help that the original name was the ARRA. But the fundamental flaw was a failed underlying narrative.

Know Your Context, Know Your Audience

Successful frames target a specific audience. They are presented by credible messengers during times and places that are relevant and understandable.

High school graduations aren't the time to give a big speech reframing Social Security and the Cartoon Network isn't the best place to do an ad buy on the "death tax."

When presenting a frame it's vital to know your context and your audience. Let's look at a few examples.

"Frankly . . . this strategy would involve us *in the wrong war, at the wrong place, at the wrong time, and with the wrong enemy.*"

When was this said and who said it?

If you guessed Dennis Kucinich you might be right since he seems to say this about everything. But it was actually General Omar Bradley's May 15, 1951, Congressional testimony.

As Chairman of the Joint Chiefs of Staff he was speaking to General Douglas MacArthur's proposal to extend the Korean War into China.

MacArthur's proposal failed.

Why?

General Bradley clearly knew the context and audience. As the chairman of the Joint Chiefs of Staff there was no doubt his words commanded instant credibility.

And did the General also meet the other key elements of framing? Yes.

Did this effectively frame the proposal with an emotional impact? Absolutely. The repetition of the word "wrong" draws a strong emotional response.

How about relevance and timeliness of the frame? Given that he was being asked his opinion about the expansion of the war before it took place, the timing and relevance couldn't have been better. His position and authority gave him the prominence and credibility to be this messenger.

And conflict? Well, the media loves conflict and there is nothing better than one general questioning another general's proposal in public. So this received a significant amount of attention.

But let's think again about Dennis Kucinich.

What if Congressman Kucinich, a strong antiwar voice and vote, had said these exact words during the debate leading up to the Iraq War? Was he the right messenger to frame the debate?

How about Senator John Kerry, a decorated war hero? Surely people would listen to him if he said this, right?

Not quite.

On September 6, 2004, while campaigning for president Senator Kerry spoke at a "front porch" event in Canonsburg, Pennsylvania. He decided to focus on the Iraq War saying, *"It's the wrong war in the wrong place at the wrong time."*

Sound familiar?

Well, it's nearly verbatim what was said more than fifty years earlier, but why didn't this framing of the Iraq War have any impact?

A few things were different.

First, Senator Kerry was speaking in America's Small Town Music Capital.

That's right. Canonsburg, a city of fewer than 10,000, has had more songs make the charts than any other small town in America. Most were recorded by Perry Como.

Why does this matter?

For starters, if you're going to make a powerful speech about the war in Iraq you may not want to do it at a "front porch" event in a city known predominately for its music.

Senator Kerry, a decorated war hero, may have had the prominence to give the speech, and the conflict was there (after all, it was a bit different from the war strategy at the time), but the campaign may have missed the mark on knowing the context and knowing the audience.

What frame could have stuck?

Canonsburg is located about eighteen miles southwest of Pittsburgh. It was a town that relied on steel mills and coal mines as the primary economic drivers. In fact, the small town's population was higher in the 1920 census than in the 2010 census. A number of the mills shut down and even the daily newspaper had closed about a decade earlier.

Yet the unemployment rate is lower than the national average. And *Money* magazine even named it one of the best places to live in the United States. The underlying narrative in Canonsburg wasn't one with above-average concern about the war—it was about the American story of struggle and rebirth.

This was an opportunity to talk about bread and butter issues: an economic theme.

For frames to work the context needs to be relevant. Your audience needs to be receptive to the frame you are presenting. It can have emotional components and contrast, but up against a differing narrative and in a context that doesn't make sense, it is bound to fall flat.

Facts are Passé

And you will know the truth, and the truth will set you free.
John 8:32

If it's good enough for scripture it should be good enough for communications strategy. But it turns out that facts have become irrelevant.

How often have you tried to rationalize with a loved one using only facts?

If you're like me you've done it all of the time. And if you're like me you've failed pretty much all of the time.

Why is this?

Professor George Lakoff, the father of modern framing, has noted that people don't think in terms of facts—they think in terms of emotional frames. Facts must fit into these frames or they don't resonate.

No matter how much I wish it were the case, facts alone aren't the solution to effectively reaching your audience.

According to Lakoff, "Neuroscience tells us that each of the concepts we have, the long-term concepts that structure how we think, is instantiated in the synapses of our brain." These concepts cannot be changed by someone simply telling us a fact.

He points out that although we may be presented with facts, for us to make sense of them, "they have to fit what is already in the synapses of the brain." Put simply, they need to fit within the established narrative that has been created by the individual.

So what does this mean for framing?

It means that when you are communicating you need to focus on the emotional components of the message. This *does not* mean that you ignore the facts or make things up to support your viewpoint. Rather, it means that your frame should resonate at an emotional level.

Think back to the conversation with your loved one. Sure, it may have been *rational* not to have purchased the trip to Hawaii that was advertised in the Sunday travel section. After all, your family couldn't afford it. But the reason you are having a conversation about it is because your loved one purchased it anyway.

By simply arguing the fact pattern about not being able to afford it you and I both know you are going to lose. Leading with "this is two times what we make in a month" may be factually correct but it isn't a strong way to frame your argument.

Instead, the framing needs to have an *emotional* component to resonate.

Remember the term anchoring—when people rely too heavily on one piece of information when making decisions?

No one said this one piece of information has to be factual. In fact, it more than likely connects on an emotional level rather than a rational level.

Loved One saw an ad in the Sunday travel section that sounded like a good deal based on—or anchored on—some arbitrary piece of information so . . . voila! It was purchased!

Lakoff suggests speaking of *values* rather than facts-only methods and using *empathy* and *responsibility* as guiding principles. Although he focuses on political messaging, this model applies to the business world and even the personal realm, as in the Hawaii discussion with your loved one.

Reflecting back on the yogurt commercial frame, you'll recall that the ad doesn't present the facts—"35 percent of our consumers will lose 3 pounds in 2 months while 25 percent will lose 5 pounds in 2 months." Saying these facts would have no emotional resonance.

But focusing on the product's role in helping you get bathing suit ready says the same factual thing in a much more emotionally compelling way.

Lakoff notes that in his inaugural address President Obama worked to reframe some policy issues in terms of values. Using the inaugural speech as a guide Lakoff points out how Obama used empathy and responsibility as key framing themes throughout:

Empathy: "The kindness to take in a stranger when the levees break, the selflessness of workers who would rather cut their hours than see a friend lose their job, the firefighter's courage to storm a stairway filled with smoke, but also a parent's willingness to nurture a child . . ."

Responsibility: "[Those] values upon which our success depends, upon honesty and hard work, courage and fair play . . ." "We have duties to ourselves, the nation, and the world . . ." "There is nothing so satisfying to the spirit, so defining of character, than giving our all to a difficult task."

President Obama could have spoken in terms of facts such as the number of volunteer hours that people had given during crises or the number of workers that took furloughs to save other's jobs.

But it was more powerful to speak to the issues in terms of empathy and emotion.

Don't Accept the Incoming Frame

So now that you know how to construct a solid frame you should also know how to avoid one that is coming your way.

Ever had to speak to the media about an issue that has faced your business or your campaign? Did you feel like they were asking you a question when they already had a predisposition toward a certain answer?

I'm sure the answer is yes but before you write off the media it's important to look at how you respond to ways in which "framed" questions come your way.

As American University communications professor Matthew Nisbet has written, in storytelling, communicators can select from a collection of interpretations. The storyteller's preferred meanings are filtered by the predispositions of the audience that shape their judgments and decisions.

The media is no different.

They are both the initial audience and the eventual storyteller. Sure, we'd *like* to think of everyone in the media as nonbiased and unable to be influenced by frames. And I think that many journalists truly do work hard to ensure this is the case.

But the reality is that journalists are people too and they have opinions and use frames to simplify complex issues just as much as the rest of your target audience does. After all, how else would they make sense of a subject they had just learned about that day and then turn around and interpret it to thousands of people?

When you are presenting information to the media you want to do it in the same way you would any other target audience—develop a narrative and core message, and frame the issue.

But when the media comes at you with a frame how do you counter it?

One way *not* to do it, unless you want to be famous on the blogosphere, is to challenge the interviewer, get angry, and say, "listen [enter expletive here], why are you wasting my time if you are just going to write the article you want to write anyway?"

It might be fun to do that but it won't really help out the article.

First, to counter the incoming frame the most important thing is not to repeat or accept the frame. Think about a recent newspaper article you have read. When you saw the quotes from one of its sources did you also see the questions that were asked to produce those quotes?

Generally the answer is no.

But if you look closely at a lot of newspaper interviews you can infer what questions the journalists have asked. That is because the interviewee accepted the journalist's frame as presented.

In your interview, since the journalists aren't writing the question down to accompany your answer, there is no need to accept the question as framed.

Before you (and journalists reading this) panic, don't forget that this stance isn't suggesting you avoid the question. This is simply saying that you are in control of the interview and should remember that just because a question is asked a certain way *does not* mean you have to answer it in the same manner.

Let's look at an example.

Say you are the owner of the small local bookstore we mentioned earlier. You will recall when we looked at narrative that the local bookstore was struggling to survive in a world of Internet pricing and massive selection; you'll also recall that it is important for the store to connect on an emotional level over data level.

But data is what the local journalist wants to focus on. After all, a new mega bookstore wants to come into town and offer cheaper prices and a cool café and the journalist knows that your sales will take a hit.

So when you have begun a signature campaign to save your bookstore from the behemoth, the local paper calls you for an interview. After exchanging some pleasantries you receive the following questions:

Journalist: I understand you've started a signature campaign to encourage the local city council to prevent MegaBooks from coming to town. Some other retailers are saying that given the lower prices they would offer you'd lose 35 percent of your business. Isn't this just a self-interested attempt to stay open?

You: *[Silently]* Oh crap.

Journalist: And to follow on that, if people want to support your small business wouldn't they still do it even if MegaBooks opens? Isn't that capitalism?

You: *[Less Silently]* Oh crap.

Does this sound familiar? It may be a little strong but it illustrates the point. What would happen if you had accepted or repeated the incoming frame? What if you had said the following:

You: This has nothing to do with our profits. I'm a firm believer in capitalism and I understand why some people would be interested in lower-cost books, but this isn't about that.

With this reply, now you have repeated and accepted the frames. Imagine how the quote will read and imagine what the framework of the story will look like. The entire story will be focused on a new bookstore coming to town with lower costs and your quotes will only support that frame.

So how would you not accept the incoming frame and possibly even pivot to your own, more emotional, compelling frame?

Let's try this answer:

You: This is fundamentally a story about David versus Goliath. I imagine a community where small independent family businesses continue to thrive because neighbors help neighbors succeed. We are a part of this community, our children go to school here, and our lives and hearts are here. We view our bookstore as an extension of our home and want our community to continue to be welcomed into our business as though it were their second home.

Now imagine the possible headline: "MegaBooks Seen as Goliath Taking on David."

You didn't avoid the question that was asked; you just provided a new, more emotionally compelling frame.

Note also how the response doesn't focus on the percentage of lost sales or the price advantages of MegaBooks or anything else that will lose your audience's interest.

The numbers are inherent in the image of David taking on Goliath. The big guy has the advantages and you are trying to create an emotional picture as to why the little guy should win.

Media frames work because they connect the mental dots for the public. The public already has an underlying narrative about the small bookstore and MegaBooks. It's up to you to guide the media frames so the audience (both the journalist and the readers) come away with a better understanding of what information is being presented.

Now Go Do It

Framing is used to present the same information in different ways. The media, politicians, teachers and parents all use frames to help explain information.

Scientists have shown that people organize information into frames as a way to understand complex issues or simply to connect the dots between things they know and what they are being presented with. In other words, frames resonate at an emotional and understandable level. These frames build off of a narrative that you've already established and that your audience already understands.

Remember the key elements of successful frames:

> Emotional Impact
> Relevance and Ease of Understanding

> ➤ Conflict (does it create two clear sides and provide contrast?)

As opposed to simply using facts to frame your argument, speak instead in a way that has emotional resonance. Try framing with something that speaks to your values, use empathy, and choose words that emotionally connect.

Have you ever been in a media interview and felt the interviewer already had his or her mind made up regarding their position? Has the interviewer ever asked you questions that seemed leading or "framed?"

Here are some simple tips for dealing with this situation:

➤ Don't accept or repeat the incoming frame
➤ Present your narrative and core message
➤ Pivot to your compelling counterframe

Framing is an essential communications tool. But it can't stand alone. You need to build up a strong narrative and core message and then frame from that point. If you use these tools you will be able to more effectively communicate with your targeted audience.

CHAPTER 7

SOCIAL MEDIA

Gresham's Law

In the sixteenth century social media consisted of word-of-mouth excitement over the Gutenberg Bible. After all, the world was just fifty years into the idea of the printing press and it was pretty exciting that six books could print simultaneously.

But the idea that one day we would be digitally speaking with ampersands in order to stick within our allotted 140 Twitter character limit was as far-flung as space travel.

Yet, the sixteenth century did produce something, or someone, that tells us how to use social media effectively: Sir Thomas Gresham.

Sir Thomas Gresham was credited with noting that "bad money drives out good." Or, when you have two commodities, the artificially overvalued item will drive out the artificially undervalued item.

Modern economists and social scientists have grown to view "Gresham's Law" as applicable to information—a commodity during the current information age.

Hal Varian, an economist and author, believes that Gresham's Law of Information would mean "bad information crowds out good." Or, "low-quality, cheap information can displace high-quality, authoritative information."

How does this apply to your personal narrative or brand and what does this tell you about social media?

Let's take a political campaign for example.

Unlimited access to partisan blog and websites, social media, talk radio, and political punditry on TV can often displace high-quality information—replacing it with low-quality information that is passed off as the good stuff. As this information gets continuously passed on, it becomes normalized and accepted as *The Word.*

We're all guilty of this. A little Internet surfing using some key words to find information on questionable blogs that support what we want to believe?

Yep.

I've done it.

And it turns out that so have millions of other people, and it's having an impact on who we vote for, what businesses we support, and even whether we get hired for a job (I *knew* I shouldn't have posted *that* photo of myself on Facebook!).

Every day we have nearly unlimited access to information, a lot of it coming from social media. Some of it is good and some of it is less than or equal to good.

Determining which of it is low-quality information displacing high-quality information can be a difficult task. We are seeing low-quality information in politics, business, and even education.

That's right, just when you were hoping that this type of information crowding was only occurring in the political discourse it turns out educators are noticing this as well.

When I was in school my teachers said they read CliffsNotes just to prevent us from using CliffsNotes in our papers. I always thought that was clever . . . albeit a bit mean.

Now teachers are claiming that their students are referencing the Internet too heavily and extracting more bad information than good. Tara Brabazon, Professor of Media at the University of Brighton, believes the Internet is "flattening expertise" because every piece of information is given the same credibility by users.

As Joshua Finnell, a reference librarian who has written on Gresham's Law, notes, "The first result in a search engine is by no means the most authoritative, but it is the most convenient. The puzzled professor who finds well-researched papers a scarcity need look no further than the Internet to see that good information is at a premium and that bad information is pushing it to the fringes."

From CliffsNotes to Wikipedia and from partisan blogs to the twenty-four-hour news cycle, low-quality information abounds. [Note: I promise I used Wikipedia fewer than a dozen times for this book].

But how do you break out of this cycle and actually reach your audience with high-quality information?

It Was Nice to Meet You

Recently a friend of mine had a terrible customer service experience. The kind that was so bad he thought at any moment the *Candid Camera* crew would jump out from behind the counter and everyone would all have a laugh.

Unfortunately, that didn't happen.

So being a good citizen he decided to go home and blast the place on Yelp.

Fair?

Maybe.

Common?

Yes.

Businesses face the same problem that educators and candidates face: a significant amount of easily available, low-quality information. Yelpers, like my friend, sometimes take imperfect or limited information and print it as *The Word*.

This information becomes the basis for decision making on what restaurants to eat at, which hotels to stay, at or even which candidates to vote for.

I'm proud to say I'm 100 percent guilty of this.

I won't stay at a hotel before I've checked rating sites and when I'm in a new town Yelp is my go-to for restaurant reviews.

And there is value in having these types of reviews—just as long as we realize that some of them actually contain low-quality information. And not just from patrons, but also from the businesses themselves.

Thanks to the widespread availability of information, from ratings sites to blog reviews, businesses have found a need for a whole new subindustry of image management.

That's right, businesses hire people to counter the emotional responses of people like my buddy who blast them on Yelp. After all, the last thing a business wants is a poor review on a ratings site or a negative blog article placing high in search results. So a number of businesses actually hire firms to create their own blog reviews, take their own photos, or submit their own ratings.

This means that they rig rigged information.

Some of it is fair given that many of us don't provide positive or thorough reviews when we have a good experience at a hotel or restaurant (therefore skewing the data unfairly toward the negative). But some of it is simply replacing poor information with additional poor information.

But assuming you don't have public relations firms at your beck and call, or you actually want to do this the old-fashioned way and earn it, how do you break through the "cheap information" and replace it with good?

Noted political scientist Samuel Popkin at the University of California, San Diego, may have the answer.

Popkin believes that a small amount of personal information can drive out a large amount of impersonal information, because personal information is much more helpful to your audience as they form their own opinions.

Therefore any person or business, regardless of what is theoretically "known" about them, has an opportunity to paint a relevant picture of information for their audience.

Especially if the information provided is personal and emotional; the candidate or business will be able to inverse Gresham's Law and crowd out "low-quality" information and replace it with smaller amounts of "authoritative" information.

Think about it. When was the last time you had an encounter with a celebrity, or a political candidate, or someone else who is well known to the public? Overwhelmingly, that short and personal encounter crowded out all other chatter you heard about that person and allowed you to form your own opinion. And that opinion is generally positive.

Or maybe you have stayed at a hotel and read some reviews in Trip Advisor that terrified you but after experiencing the people and place personally, you had a different view.

Face-to-face contact—"it was nice to meet you!" has greater influence than a simple social media posting.

This is a key point.

You have the ability to influence and connect with your audience, thereby replacing low-quality information with *The Real Word*.

Knowing from Gresham's Law that low-quality information can crowd out high-quality information, you can fight back by providing personal connections that override even large amounts of low-quality information.

The most effective social media campaigns provide a personal and emotional connection to the end user.

Everyone Is an Author

Now before you panic and think that I'm saying all social media, blogs, partisan websites, and talk shows are bad things, let me say you're only *partially* right.

We live in an age where everyone can be an author.

Remember when Walter Cronkite was *the* news?

Well, Walter now looks like thousands of people in their basements and living rooms producing content. News no longer flows from few to many, as it did when the network television stations and large print papers dominated, but from many to many.

We can be honest: A lot of what we see produced by the living room authors is less than desirable (read *crap*). But some of it has broken major stories, shaped the way we've looked at difficult events (like natural disasters and poverty), and even given us firsthand information about celebrities and politicians that the mainstream news didn't (or wouldn't) cover.

In the modern media age one of the most powerful tools is an effective and emotionally connective social media campaign. But social media's power has the ability to be manipulated with a high amount of low-quality information that is passed off as the real thing.

In his seminal (but disturbing) book entitled *Trust Me, I'm Lying,* Ryan Holiday explains how he used social media to shape traditional media coverage. He effectively created fake content and controversies, pushed it through social media, and made it "real" by having traditional media cover it.

The way that Holiday explains it, "Blogs have enormous influence over other blogs, making it possible to turn a post on a site with only little traffic into posts on much bigger sites." Because blogs compete to "get stories first, newspapers compete to confirm it and then pundits compete for airtime to opine on it."

This method of "trading up the chain" allows stories that are pushed through secondary social media sites to become covered as *The Word* by traditional media. Holiday noted that he did this in manipulative ways to drive sales for his clients of books, movies, and even clothing.

He found small blogs that would bite on covering his false stories and even advised nonprofit executives on how to make viral videos that are pushed through the right channels to drive money to their charities.

As a result, he helped produced large quantities of low-quality information that was covered as the good stuff by the nightly news.

Holiday acknowledges there are vulnerabilities in the system that can be done for good or the opposite of good. But he provides some nuggets of media context that can help you or your business reach your audience in an honest way.

Remember everyone is an author. And the traditional media, such as your local newspaper or television station, is in a constant battle to break news before their competition can—so much so that they rely on "everyone is an author" to do the work for them. Holiday knows that journalists are relying on these "authors" as valid sources.

According to a study by George Washington University, 89 percent of journalists reported using blogs for their research for stories. That means 89 percent of the people at your local newspaper and television station are using blogs manipulated by people like Holiday to produce "legitimate" news.

Let me be the first to point out the obvious: This sucks.

But it's also reality.

So how do you play within this game in an honest way? How do you take advantage of this system of high-quality outlets using low-quality information?

You must replace the low-quality information with small amounts of authoritative, connective (emotional/personal) information that is traded up the chain.

Let's look at the steps:

> Find influential blogs or social media sites that are frequently "traded up the chain," such as the *Huffington Post,* Gawker, BuzzFeed, Drudge Report, reddit, and Twitter. Find sites that traditional news sites reference, as those are generally the most influential.
> Provide your information to these sites or to even smaller (sometimes local) sites that these sites use to search for information.
> Once coverage is obtained through the influential blogs or social media sites be sure to pitch and push this information to traditional media.

So how do you do this?

Let's say you have a nonprofit and you're trying to get coverage for an event you are putting on. We've all complained to our local news that they don't cover anything that is newsworthy.

One way to do it is to send a press release out to the local media and hope for the best. This method is the most common and also equates to what those in the business call "failure."

That isn't actually an inside term—it just sounds like something the media world would say.

Another way to do it, generally with more success, is to "pitch" the local media. This would involve calling up or e-mailing personal contacts at the local media to "pitch" your story, answering the following common questions in your pitch:

Why is it newsworthy?

Why should it displace the "if it bleeds it leads" story?

What is the angle?

In other words, how much of the story can you write for the journalist so that she doesn't have to worry about your story among the three to five stories she has to write that day?

The last thing you could do, as discussed previously, to get your event covered is to force traditional media coverage through gaining buzz with smaller, social media sites.

Meaning, you could actually drive what your local papers and television stations cover and even *how they frame* the story by using a social media or nontraditional outlet first.

So back to your nonprofit event. Let's say its purpose is to raise money for kids to see how laws (and sausage) are made in Washington, D.C.

We can be honest: On the face of it, this isn't an interesting story.

If you were the editor of the local newspaper there doesn't seem to be a reason to displace the grizzly bear attack on a fisherman from the front page.

But what if you could find a way to provide a small amount of emotional, connective, and authoritative information that the editor would feel compelled to cover? Or what if you had already created local buzz through other social media means that forced her to cover it so the paper wasn't left out?

So your local newspaper doesn't want to cover it?

No problem—push it to local blogs. In fact, write it for them. Do your own interviews and tell your own story. Frame it the way you want to frame it. Create your own narrative about the kids' trip to Washington D.C.

Find an emotionally compelling narrative from the perspective of one of the kids going on the trip. Maybe that kid is the first in his family to visit D.C. Maybe he is the first to be in an airplane. Maybe he just became a citizen last week.

Whatever it is, make it connect emotionally with the readers.

Which blogs do you push it to?

Maybe there is a local blog that is followed by your local newspapers. Maybe one of the parents in the group is a blogger for the

Huffington Post or even keeps his or her own local blog.

Once they publish your story—and they will—e-mail that story to your network of friends, Tweet it, post it on Facebook, and distribute it to all of the parents who have kids going to Washington, D.C.

And then have a few people e-mail the story to your local news outlets.

The local news will cover it. And they will most likely cover it in the way that you were hoping for.

Everyone Is a Videographer

Forty-eight hours of footage every minute.

That is the amount of video uploaded to YouTube every day.

Most businesses and campaigns know they need to be providing video content and engaging through YouTube. But what is the most effective way to break through the hundreds of thousands of hours of content?

It better stir your audience's emotions.

As Ryan Holiday points out, the most "powerful predictor of whether content will spread online is valence, or the degree of positive or negative emotion a person is made to feel."

So the more that your video can invoke emotion, the more it is likely to be spread online.

I'm not necessarily advocating for businesses to create videos that tick off their audiences, although it seems to work, as was seen in the most viral video of all time—KONY 2012.

KONY 2012, a thirty-minute documentary about Ugandan rebel leader Joseph Kony, was seen 100 million times in only six days. According to Visible Measures, a social media digital metrics company, this made it the most viral video of all time.

Why did the video take off?

It had the "valence" to resonate in a negative way.

As the *L.A. Times* notes, KONY 2012 "exploded into public consciousness as a rare bird: an Internet video that captivated the multitudes with a story of geopolitics and human suffering, not a pop diva's star turn."

But it wasn't just the human suffering that made the video viral, it was also the controversy around the piece itself. The *L.A. Times* noted that "critics said the video had oversimplified and distorted the story of Joseph Kony and the Lord's Resistance Army, or LRA, which has kidnapped children and turned them into sex slaves and boy soldiers for more than a quarter of a century."

The story about the video made it even more viral as traditional news outlets, like the *L.A. Times,* picked up the story and ran with it.

Did the spread of the video work?

According to one human rights exec, Jan Egeland, it did. She noted that many groups, including the United Nations, "struggled for years to bring attention to Kony's atrocities and slowly built a consensus to stop him." But this viral video was "a big net plus" in encouraging the discussion.

Ultimately, their video succeeded because it:

➤ Connected emotionally
➤ Provided a call to action
➤ Started with a compelling narrative

As Danah Boyd, a social media researcher told the *New York Times,* the video production company that made KONY "create[s] narratives that can be boiled down to 140 characters while still engaging people emotionally. They create action messages that can be encapsulated into a hashtag. And they already have a strong network of people who are, by and large, young, passionate, active on social media, and structurally disconnected from one another."

She said that last part was most important because it means the message can be inserted into a diverse range of youth conversations all at once, exponentially expanding its reach.

The *New York Times* notes that Jason Russell, the film's director and narrator, provides a direct call to action, asking "viewers to join him in this campaign to capture Mr. Kony after describing his friendship with one of Mr. Kony's victims and then sharing a compelling narrative about how he became involved in this effort."

Once people began to get engaged, the video spread from celebrities to traditional media—becoming a household video in less than a week.

But not all viral videos need to touch on anger.

So how do you emotionally connect and create a viral video using other elements?

One way to do it is to let your kids do the talking (or laughing).

Marcus McArthur was an unemployed graduate student in American history at St. Louis University in Missouri. He was sorting through the mail as his eight-month-old son, Micah, looked on.

In the collection of mail he came across a rejection letter for a job that he had applied for. When he slowly ripped up the rejection letter in front of his son, young Micah burst into laughter.

Dad grabbed his video camera and filmed a video of Micah that was less than two minutes. His son's laughter, and the irony of what his son was laughing at, caught YouTube by storm. The original video has been seen more than 45 million times on YouTube.

Marcus's video connected emotionally. It made people laugh but it also connected in a different way. Many of us have been rejected for jobs, dates, and even Publisher's Clearing House millions.

Rejection isn't easy. It is something we have all emotionally grappled with.

But for eight-month-old Micah? Not so much.

The ripping envelope was just a funny sound to him and his laughter at the rejection allowed us to connect with the video and the story behind the video in a unique way.

It had all the ingredients of being a viral hit.

Now that you've seen two examples of successful YouTube videos, let's create a viral video together.

Dr. Annie Lang, a professor in the Department of Telecommunications at Indiana University and an expert in developing media images that stick, has provided some suggestions for making your video stand out.

- ➤ **Let the emotions talk:** Emotion compels attention and engages the viewer. Dr. Lang notes that numerous studies confirm that people remember emotional stories better than dull ones.
- ➤ **Slow it down:** Just like you can't understand your super-excited kid talking at a million words a minute, neither

can your audiences understand an extremely fast-paced, verbose, and complex video.

➤ **Engage your viewers:** Create videos that tell stories in the same way you would tell them in person. Provide a call to action, an engagement. Dr. Lang encourages people to use strong, chronological narratives and not to make viewers search their memories in order to understand your story.

Low Information Rationality

Given the crush of information available to your audience, through social media, blogs, and the twenty-four-hour news cycle, does this mean people are actually more informed than previous generations?

Most likely not.

As noted above, too much low-quality information has been crowding out the good stuff.

So we work to create personal connections with people, even in the social media world, to push back with higher-quality information.

But assuming you don't have the ability to interact personally with your target audience, what is another way to break through the low-quality information?

Samuel Popkin, whom we cited earlier in regard to personal information driving out impersonal information, has a powerful theory on this as well, and one that can truly shape how to construct narratives in a social media world.

He's deemed it "low information rationality."

These aren't exactly Twitter optimized terms but the theory will make sense in a second.

Coined by Popkin, "low information rationality" is used help explain how voters reach electoral decisions, even without great knowledge of individual candidates. In essence, voters use small amounts of personal information to construct a narrative about candidates.

Put simply, people infer.

James Carville and Paul Begala, the architects behind Bill Clinton's successful (if improbable) run for the presidency in 1991, tell a story of another client they had in order to illustrate Popkin's theory.

We once had this candidate that was endorsed by the gay community, who was a strong environmentalist and was very pro-union. If we gave you that information, and nothing more, and then we asked you what you thought his position on abortion rights was you'd say pro-choice. And you'd be wrong. That client was the late Pennsylvania governor Bob Casey. Why would you infer he was pro-choice? None of the issues had any logical linear connection to abortion.

People infer based on intuition, media coverage, narratives created by political parties and businesses, what their friends say, and more. From the example above, if you asked 100 voters whether the candidate was pro-choice, you'd most likely get 100 voters telling you that he was.

Information, Popkin argues, is a byproduct of people's activities on a day-to-day basis and their interactions with information sources such as social media. Taking all of this disparate information allows us to make seemingly informed choices about candidates or businesses even when we have imperfect information.

So how do you use this theory to help shape your social media outreach?

The information you provide via social media should help your audience *infer your targeted message.*

This might sound complex but let's look at an example to see how it is done.

In the 1991/92 presidential campaign, James Carville and Paul Begala knew that the standing narrative about Bill Clinton, formed from limited information, was that he had been accused of dodging the draft while attending elite Ivy League schools and heading to England as a Rhodes Scholar. Carville and Begala noted that

[Voters] took these stars and created a constellation of a spoiled, rich brat that never had to work for anything in life. Voters initially thought Clinton was a product of privilege: a trust fund baby who dodged the draft and tooled around in his daddy's convertible and had no sense of what their lives or their struggles were about.

So the campaign went about to add additional "stars to the constellation," as they called it.

They began telling stories about a boy from Hope, Arkansas, about how his mom had been widowed, and his grandparents had taken care of him while his mother studied to be a nurse. Clinton spoke of finding his inspiration for public service as a young boy after meeting President Kennedy thirty years earlier and working his way through college.

Essentially, the Clinton campaign took Popkin's theory and created a narrative that allowed voters to infer.

They contrasted President Bush, with a Kennebunkport, Maine, compound, to the kid from Hope, Arkansas. They used personal stories to create an overarching narrative that was reinforced with everything they did and led voters to infer one thing about their candidate and another about their opponent.

How would you use the theory of low information rationality in a modern social media world?

Imagine YouTube first person narratives about the difficulty of finding work in this economy. Twitter retweets about struggling small towns but with individual stories of perseverance. How about pushing these stories to local blogs and watching as the national narrative becomes about who is more in touch with the workforce?

Think voters will choose Kennebunkport or Hope?

They will infer Hope.

If you want your narrative to be about the all-American boy done right, and a message that your guy is the person that is "in-touch" enough to solve the economic crisis or other widespread ills, then your social media components should provide inferences that help lead your audience to these narrative elements on their own.

Mozilla and the Cluetrain Manifesto

There is nothing that gets people's attention like calling something a manifesto. In 1999, a set of authors who have worked at IBM, Sun Microsystems, the *Linux Journal,* and NPR published a book (manifesto) of ninety-five theses of what they felt defined the new marketplace.

Their conclusion? That there has been a shift of power from the companies to the individuals. "A powerful global conversation has begun," they wrote. "Through the Internet, people are discovering and inventing new ways to share relevant knowledge with blinding speed."

Similar to the Yelp example from an earlier section it is hard to directly control information online in the same way that businesses can control advertising messages.

As Deirdre Breakenridge, author of *PR 2.0*, notes, brands lose their ability to control what is said about them within online communities so instead they need to focus more on pleasing their existing customers to make sure they are evangelizing, not griping. "As a result there will be a new focus on helping companies engage in information-rich, two-way conversations with their customers."

In other words, companies need to try to join the conversation in the social media world just as they would in the offline world. Providing personal contact (a form of "face-to-face" in the online world) and credibility are key to succeeding. Online they need to engage customers in deep and meaningful ways to ensure success of the service or product.

Let's look at an example.

With the shift of power to the individual some companies are realizing that engaging the customer, developing buy-in, and establishing an emotional connection can create a strong social media cycle that leads to real success on and offline.

The Firefox Web browser is a strong example of this model.

As explained by Neal Gorenflo, an expert on the use of social network analysis in business notes, it was an open-source software community that created Firefox, a volunteer effort with support from the Mozilla Foundation.

How did Firefox succeed if it was an all-volunteer effort?

"Like all open-source projects," Gorenflo said, "Firefox relied on social media to coordinate volunteer efforts. Naturally it was promoted in a way consistent with open-source production methods."

This means the promotional work was distributed to volunteers using social media and each did their small part in promotion, which added up to a large promotional campaign.

"The Spread Firefox campaign was a hugely successful, volunteer-

powered marketing campaign [that] shows how social media and engaging customers in a meaningful way in the whole product lifecycle
can create serious competitive advantages."

How successful was it?

Firefox is now one of the three most used browsers in the United
States garnering about 20 percent of market share. Imagine taking on
Microsoft's Internet Explorer, the largest and most established browser
on the current market, through an all-volunteer-led social media
campaign.

The makers of the Firefox browser weren't just included in the
conversation—they *were* the conversation. The developers and social media marketers created an emotional connection to the product.
They were engaged and wanted Firefox to succeed.

Had the Firefox team decided they would push their browser simply through traditional advertising and establishing a Facebook page
it's unlikely they would have achieved the same response. Because
they recognized that the power had shifted toward the individual,
Firefox, in many ways, established the functional equivalent of an
offline grassroots movement.

The News Cycle: 21 Minutes?

During the heat of a political campaign people can say and do things
that they regret. Historically, the degree by which these gaffes were
magnified depended on whether the traveling press corps actually
noticed them.

Given that a lot of interactions used to take place outside of the
earshot of the press, a candidate was able to get away with a lot.

Today? Not so much.

Since everyone is an author or videographer you can pretty much
guarantee that a candidate will be reminded of something he said the
minute he logs on to his computer.

Mitt Romney learned this the hard way during a 2012 campaign
stop in Commerce, Michigan, nearly two months before the election. He
dubbed the stop a "homecoming rally" because he had grown up nearby.

At 12:23 P.M. local time Romney made an off-the-cuff remark about Barack Obama's birth certificate.

"No one's ever asked to see my birth certificate," Romney told a rally of some 7,000 people in his home state of Michigan. "They know that this is the place that we were born and raised."

Hence began the twenty-one-minute news cycle and display of the power of social media.

According to the political news website Politico, the first Tweet about the comment came from the *Washington Post* at 12:23 P.M., less than sixty seconds after Romney made the remark.

"Immediately, Tweets with the phrase 'birth certificate' went from no more than five-per-minute to 138-per-minute in a matter of four minutes," they reported.

At 12:27 Politico had a short article about it on their website and at 12:28 the first video of the remark appeared on YouTube. At 12:36 the first cable news network reported on the remark.

By 12:41 the Romney campaign had issued a response clarifying the remark.

To close the loop, twenty-one minutes after the initial statement, the Obama campaign issued a statement accusing Romney of enlisting "himself in the birther movement."

And so goes the new social media reality and the twenty-one-minute news cycle—from gaffe to coverage to clarification all in under thirty minutes.

As Politico notes, the social media–driven news cycle seems to move at the speed of light. "While reporters fought to Tweet and post the story as fast as possible, the Romney campaign rushed to put out the fire while the Obama campaign sought to stoke it."

As we continue to live in a more social media–driven world it is even more important to ensure that you have a strong established narrative to counter these short news cycle bursts. In the case of the birth certificate remark, the total story came in and out of traditional media coverage (daily newspapers, nightly news) in a day. One of the reasons for its being short-lived is that the Obama team had released his birth certificate some time before and many other opposing political leaders, including John McCain and even Romney himself, had said the birth certificate issue was settled.

In other words, voters had enough personal information about the subject to reject the social media news burst. Voters inferred that this wasn't true and the story was settled. The result?

A story that ultimately lasted twenty-one minutes.

"Social" Science

In social media, people still matter.

In a world filled with low-quality information the social media campaigns that stick the most are those that spur conversations. In other words, they still need to have a human component.

Much research has been dedicated to the inner workings of social networks, and some of the most relevant findings are not new.

In fact, one of the preeminent studies was done in the 1950s by two Columbia University professors, Paul Lazarsfeld and Elihu Katz, who wrote a book on social networks and advertising called *Personal Influence*. But how it is applies to modern social media is new. And the findings of Lazarsfeld and Katz are relevant to how you should view your own social media campaigns.

"[Lazarsfeld and Katz] found that advertising was ineffective at directly changing consumer preferences and prompting purchase," Ed Keller and Brad Fay note in their book *The Face-to-Face Book*. Rather, it was effective because of how it reached "opinion leaders" who were able to persuade through personal contact and influence.

This means your social media strategy isn't about simply being present on social networking sites.

And you know what I'm talking about.

We've all heard people say, "Let's get on Twitter and Facebook and the people will come!"

That isn't a strategy.

Your presence and plan on these networks needs to connect with people so the people actually *carry* your message throughout their own social networks.

Social media helps you reach the influencers. It is the influencers (the human component) that actually make things succeed in the social media world.

Keller and Fay give an excellent example of the power of influencers. In the 2000 presidential election a change of a mere 269 votes (out of more than 100 million cast) would have meant a President Gore instead of a President Bush.

The country appeared divided. Knowing that the share of the actual independent voters that campaigns could court was shrinking fast, the 2004 George W. Bush campaign strategist Matthew Dowd decided it didn't make sense to focus 75 percent of a campaign's resources on what amounted to 7 percent of the electorate.

As Keller and Fay note, Dowd realized the best way to win an election was not to reach out to the independent or swing voters, but to reach out to the influencers (or what the Bush campaign called "navigators").

"The information flow has become a flood, a torrent of messages," Dowd said, "coming at a confused, cynical public from all angles. People are turning to one another again."

Today's online influencers are working at a grassroots level, just like last century's influencers did. Dowd notes they are no longer "from the high perches of media, politics or business. The twenty-first century opinion leaders are average Americans who know lots of other average Americans, trusted souls with large social networks."

Dowd realized that these influencers would be able to *carry* the campaign's message on and offline.

So what should you do to reach the influencers?

Keller and Fay argue that a person needs to have the *means, motive,* and *opportunity* to influence other people. What does this mean?

Luckily, it doesn't mean that you simply need to track down a celebrity and hope that he or she Tweets about your new product.

Influencers can be regular people who are:

a. actively in touch with other people
b. strong consumers of information—actively seeking out new sources
c. sought out by others because their opinion is valued

What does this equate to?

Keller and Fay's research shows that about one in ten people can be deemed influencers. These "everyday" people have a dispropor-tionate impact on the marketplace.

So how do you find them?

One of the ways in the virtual world is to use a social media influ-ence-ranking service that shows a member's influence and outreach. Influence would be the ability to inspire action, like retweeting your Twitter posts. Outreach is your willingness to engage with others or spread a message.

There are a number of online services that do this, and none of them are the golden ticket, but they do provide a general guide for locating online influencers.

One of the largest is a tech company called Klout. Klout attempts to measure your ability to influence people on the Internet. Using data aggregated from social networks it determines how good you are at persuading other people to act. Klout regularly updates and every time you login to the service it provides a score of 1–100 that shows your online influence.

For example, Klout attempts to measure whether posts on Twit-ter and Facebook receive a lot of reposting and retweeting. In other words, what happens to your content after you send it out? Do your messages start conversations? Those with higher Klout scores tend to be people that have the highest engagement with their content—the online influencers.

Other services such as PeerIndex focus on how to best understand and engage your social network—in other words, finding people who are already connected (Twitter followers, Facebook friends) who are influencers.

"The people who have PeerIndexes, people active on the social web, are generating social capital, and they may be building it in ways that line up with the company's corporate mission," PeerIndex CEO Azeem Azhar told *Inc. Magazine*. "Now, we can tell you who's likely to be a net promoter of your company, who's likely to align very closely with the things your company stands for. A connection makes a lot of sense for you and a lot of sense for the recipient."

Is PeerIndex working?

Some companies are already turning to these ranking sites to tar-get influencers. Spotify, the Swedish online streaming music service, used Klout to help with their U.S. launch. Their goal was to hit music, tech, and social media influencers through Klout, give them access to their free service, and encourage them to pass it along to their friends. Within a short period of time Spotify generated more than 30,000 Tweets, hit more than 90,000 influencers, and received more than 290 million impressions. Audi used a similar method to target automotive and design influencers for the release of one of their new models; they targeted a little more than 200 influencers and ended up with over 50 million impressions stemming from those influencers.

A number of these people would be considered "everyday people" to quote Sly and the Family Stone. In fact, *The Wall Street Journal* highlighted a story of Katie Miller, a twenty-five-year-old account executive at a public relations firm who found out what it was like to be deemed an influencer.

While traveling in Las Vegas she Tweeted about the lavish buffets and posted pictures of her seats at the aquatic spectacle "Le Rêve" at the Wynn Las Vegas hotel. A week later, she received an e-mail inviting her to a lavish holiday party in Manhattan.

Ms. Miller told *The Wall Street Journal* that she had been singled out as a "high-level influencer" by the event's sponsors, including the Venetian and Palazzo hotels in Las Vegas and Klout. Since she was determined to be a social media influencer these Las Vegas hotels were eager to win her over, hoping for her continued social media support.

Klout and other similar services shouldn't be viewed as a perfect measurement tool of online influence. But they do give you a starting point at looking for online influencers. It may be that your business doesn't need someone that is an overall influencer, just someone that is influential in your sector. These people may have fewer Twitter followers or Facebook friends but they are more engaged in your specific industry. Some of these tools let you target by industry or interest as well.

But on a smaller scale you may be able to find the influencers by simply starting in your own network. Find people who are following you and look to see if they are retweeting your Twitter posts or engaging with others to spread your message. You can target those people first.

As Keller and Fay point out in the *The Face-to-Face Book*, you can't simply rely on online influence to drive public opinion or business your way. But the offline world is connected in many ways to the virtual world. The most influential in the virtual world are those who also are sought out in the offline world.

Consequently, you may find offline influencers simply by tracking down people online who truly have influence in your targeted area.

Credibility: Still Cool

In a world filled with low-quality information it can be surprising to hear that credibility still matters. But as we saw earlier the social media campaigns that stick the most are those that spur conversations; they have a human component, which improve credibility, trust, and authenticity.

Just as being a trusted source offline means people are more likely to turn to you for information, so, too, does being a trusted source online mean people are more likely to eat up your online musings.

That's right. Credibility wasn't just a fad. Credibility is *still* cool.

According to Pete Blackshaw, an author and founder of one of the web's longest-running online feedback sites, credibility is the most important driver in today's hyperviral world.

Although Blackshaw is applying his model to businesses attempting to succeed in the social media world, his principals can apply to businesses or individuals attempting to be heard over the din of information in the land of social media.

He argues that credibility has core drivers that require different strategies to come to fruition.

What are some of the key drivers?

Trust, authenticity, and a willingness to listen to your audience.

But how do you apply this in the social media world?

Let's start with listening to your audience.

Think back at all of the times you've said, "Let's get on Twitter and Facebook. The 'likes' will pour in!" After all, you thought all you needed to do was simply be present on social media and if you built it, they would come.

But what if instead you had taken some time to "listen" to the online conversations? What are people saying on Facebook about your industry? What stories are the media covering? What blogs are being linked to and what Tweets are being retweeted?

What if you took the time to observe what is working and *then* join in on those conversations? Even more important, what if you became the person who would repost credible information to your Facebook page, retweet interesting information, and link to blogs that help out your customers, friends, and targeted audience?

The end result is that you will earn the trust of those in the online world similar to how you would earn trust in the offline world. Put simply, you would become a credible source.

For example, say you have a small marketing firm. So small in fact that the firm is just you. How do you break into the social world and become recognized?

After all, because you're in marketing you *know* you need to have a social media presence. You've started a Facebook page, a Twitter page, and even hang out on Orkut, Google Plus+, LinkedIn, and a host of other sites that prove you are seriously social.

But beyond your friends and pets you don't really have much support.

Let's make you a credible source.

First, start following credible sources in your industry. Maybe there are marketing gurus you think are the bee's knees. Follow them on Twitter, subscribe to their blog feeds, and "like" them on Facebook. Start paying attention to what they are saying, who is following them, and which of their Tweets are retweeted and posts are reposted.

When you find posts or Tweets that are interesting, repost them. Become an information source for your friend network and audience. Allow yourself to become a credible source not just to your current audience but also to some of the leaders in your industry.

At this point you're not simply contributing to the high volume of low-quality information. Rather you are becoming the person in the network who can seek out high-quality information and make sure it goes viral.

Provide this information and advice for free. Become an authentic source for your audience. You will find that just like in the offline world if you're genuine, trustworthy, and willing to listen, people will deem you a credible source.

As author Pete Blackshaw points out, "Authenticity is becoming increasingly important as consumers grow more and more cynical about advertising and brands." Often your audience is asking: "Is the company real and sincere? Does it speak with a genuine voice or one that is contrived? Are its motivations pure? Does the company *truly* care about me?"

Your success in the online world depends on this authenticity and credibility. Given the crush of low-quality information, one of the best ways to break through the social media world is to become a credible source.

Now Go Do It

With the advent of the Internet, social media, and the omnipresent twenty-four-hour cable news stations, information consumption has become more complex and arguably less vetted for the end user.

However, the study of information consumption, and the process by which your audience actually decides who to vote for or what business to patronize, is still rooted in economic and social theories that are hundreds of years old.

Sir Thomas Gresham's theories of long ago, that large amounts of low-quality information can push out higher-quality information, apply today. As we are flooded with information from social networks, blogs, and more, how do we ensure that our message is heard?

And how do we pushback on low-quality information to ensure that the good stuff we want to push is noticed?

To recap, here are a few steps to achieving these goals.

Step 1:

Integrate personal information and personal contact. Personal information can drive out a large amount of impersonal information, because personal information is much more helpful to your audience's forming their own opinions.

Especially if the informational narrative is personal and emotional, the candidate or business will be able to inverse Gresham's Law and crowd out low-quality information and replace it with smaller amounts of authoritative information.

Personal and emotional connections are much more powerful than large amounts of low-quality information.

Step 2:

"Trade up the chain."

Traditional media outlets are in an all-out war to break news first. The trouble is that they are being smoked by blogs that don't follow the same journalistic cannons of excellence.

Yes, journalists have ethics.

Since traditional media don't have the ability to beat blogs and social media to the punch they often rely on those sources so they can beat other traditional media outlets.

You can take advantage of this by providing high-quality information to local or influential blogs, which can drive traditional media coverage.

Here are the steps:

➤ Find influential blogs or social media sites that are frequently "traded up the chain," such as the *Huffington Post*, Gawker, BuzzFeed, Drudge Report, reddit, and Twitter. Find sites that traditional news sites reference, as those are generally the most influential.

➤ Provide your information to these sites or to even smaller (sometimes local) sites that these sites use to search for information.

➤ Once coverage is obtained through the influential blogs or social media sites, be sure to pitch and push this information to traditional media.

Step 3:

Help people infer.

People infer based on intuition, media coverage, what their friends and family say, and more.

Because we are bombarded with loads of low-quality information our audiences need to take small cues and infer what is necessary.

Your social media and messaging strategy should help people infer. It should connect with your narrative and provide information about your business or candidate that allows them to form opinions that parallel your narrative.

Step 4:

Be a credible source.

The online world is similar to the offline world. In an online world of low-quality information, credible people have a leg up; they're rare. If you are willing to listen to the online conversations, be authentic, and post high-quality content, you will become a credible source.

Credible sources will break through the din of the social media world and will find themselves reposted, retweeted, and followed.

CONCLUSION

It was an unseasonably sunny and mild day on October 4, 2008, in Philadelphia. In exactly one month millions of voters would take to the polls to elect Barack Obama as president of the United States. On this day, however, more than 100,000 people would come to see candidate Obama at an unprecedented four rallies in one city in one day.

No candidate in recent memory had spent an entire day, one month out from an election, in one city. But Philadelphia is a special place. It is so neighborhood-centric that it is like a collection of cities within a city. A microcosm of the national electorate, The City of Brotherly Love was a test of Obama's appeal to the disparate coalition necessary to win the presidential election.

It was a little after 1 P.M. and the motorcade was making the eight-mile trip from Vernon Park in Germantown through I-76 and the streets of Philly to South 52nd and Locust. Demographically these two locations were quite different, but the response was the same.

Residents lined the streets to catch a glimpse of the candidate, forcing traffic to one lane and slowing the motorcade down to speeds that you're actually suppose to drive in neighborhoods but no one does. The staff members were busy typing on their BlackBerries sending out notes back to the campaign headquarters about turnout, media interviews, dignitary speeches, and whether there would be any food in the holding area behind the stage at the next event. In other words, we were too busy to notice the remarkable movement occurring all around.

I was in one of those vehicles when one of my co-workers told me to look up from my typing. "Something's happening," he said. "We're going to win this election."

Our day had started at 4:30 A.M. and would not let up until the senator was wheels-up early that evening. As with most campaign days this one wouldn't actually end until about 11 that night.

But right now we were more interested in taking a second to look around us than caring about what time it was. And truth be told, we still had another event where 25,000 were waiting.

As we pulled onto Locust Street to park we were surrounded by dozens of older row houses. This area had been hit hard by the economy and one of the local elected officials told us that presidential candidates don't normally stump here.

Maybe that is why hundreds of local residents lined the porches on Locust waiting for the motorcade to come to a stop. Or maybe they just wanted to see if this guy was the real deal. As the senator got out, he waved to people that were shouting for his attention, and was taken to a secure holding area.

The rest of us got out to take our places throughout the rally. I was handling the media, providing quotes and information to the dozens of traveling and local media outlets. But as I got out of the car and started to walk up Locust I heard a woman calling to me. She was sitting up on her porch overlooking the spectacle. She was African American, appeared to be in her eighties, and had a cane and glasses but an easy smile.

"Son," she said, "come up here so I can tell you something."

Now if you've ever worked on a campaign you dread these moments. After all, in the last dozen or so rallies I had done, this gesture normally equated with being given some sort of handmade trinket to give to the senator or his wife. (My favorite? A 2XL bedazzled shirt for Mrs. Obama that contained a handmade image of her and the senator. "She will love it!" the gift giver implored to me, "I can see her wearing it at the next event!" Well, I don't pretend to know if the Obamas are bedazzlers, but I do know that no one wears 2XL in that household.)

So I figured this was the same thing.

But the media overheard this call-out so the last thing I was going to do was become a negative story on an overwhelmingly positive media day. Up the stairs I trudged and asked how I could help her.

"Son," she said, "come closer." She took my hand and arm and pulled me closer to her seated position.

"I want you to know something," she said softly. "I never thought I would live long enough to see the day that a bright young white man like yourself would be working to elect the first black president." She paused.

"But I'm glad I did . . . thank you, thank you, thank you. You don't know how much this means."

We both started to cry.

I was working on a little more than three hours of sleep but it didn't matter. She told me something that I will remember for the rest of my life. She told me a story, a narrative. It had emotion, it had a plot, and it had characters. There was so much that she said without saying it.

I can assume she wasn't a media professional or a CEO. She hadn't been through corporate training courses on what to say and how to say it. And I can't imagine she figured she'd have the opportunity to speak to someone in the campaign just by sitting on her porch that day.

But she knew how to tell a story. She knew how to make it real.

There are a handful of moments in your life when things resonate so strongly, and connect so much that they seem to take you to the next act in your life's play.

These things all stem from narrative and emotion. And to the woman on Locust Street, whose name I do not know, I have to say this: "No, thank *you.*"

ACKNOWLEDGMENTS

"Before I had first done so, writing a book seemed a fine, even grand thing. And so it still seems—except, truth to tell, it is a lot better to have written a book than to actually be writing one."—Joseph Epstein

Let me tell you something, Joseph, you're spot on.

Writing a book takes qualities that my wife would correctly say I possess in limited quantities: specifically the patience of Job and great attention to detail.

This book wouldn't have been possible without others filling in those limits.

First, thank you to my wife, Tina, to whom this book is dedicated. I cannot think of someone else who would be willing to give up most of a Hawaiian vacation so I could write and then rewrite chapters.

Thank you to my parents, Peter and Cynthia, for their love, wisdom, and belief that if I wanted to do it then it *shall* be done. Thank you to my brothers, sisters, nieces, and nephews who accept the fact that this will be their stocking stuffer.

Thank you to my grandmother who spent time calling me to ensure that I knew all of my spelling words a few decades ago. Grandma, I love you and appreciate it but am glad for spell check.

Thank you to my literary agent, Dana Newman, for helping me refine a raw idea and turn it into polished project. Her advice was always desired and always incorporated.

Thank you to everyone at the Turner Publishing family, Todd

Bottorff, Diane Gedymin, and Christina Roth for believing in the project and guiding me through the process.

Thank you to Spencer Critchley, a frequent writing partner, for your advice, humor, and support and for reminding me that stories matter.

Thank you to Geoffrey Dunn and Christine Brainerd for reviewing the chapters, providing edits, and reminding me that sentence structure matters.

Thank you to Donnie Fowler, Sean Smith, Ryan Coonerty, Debbie Mesloh, Lizz Winstead, Amanda Crumley, and Leslie Miller for being my connections to the outside world throughout this project.

Thank you to John and Sheri Shull, Mike, Cathy and Ellen Shull, Becky Nix, Aunt Leslie, the Ovadias, Kevin and Bev Vogel, Rick Martinez, Steve Clark, Dick Wilson, Scott Collins, Dave Price, Ben Reed, Jeff Keisel, Peter Koht, Kris Reyes, Paul Shone, Caleb Baskin, George Mohler, Jeff Brantingham, Bobby Whithorne, Adam Abrams, Kristen Lee, Walter Shapiro, Chris Matthews, Jamal Simmons, Patrick Mulhearn, Allyson Violante, Ben Glatt, Fran Church, Pat Emard, Carol Fuller, and Kim Balin for your friendship, advice, and lunches.

And to all the people I forgot, take to Twitter to let the world know.

A good portion of research for this book was done at Santa Clara University and the University of California, Santa Cruz. Parts of this book were written in Santa Cruz County, Santa Clara, San Diego, Seattle, Nashville, Boise, Kauai, and on the planes that took me there.

NOTES

Chapter 1: Narrative

Bennis, W. "The Leader as a Storyteller." *Harvard Business Review*, January 1996.

Chicago Public Media. *This American Life*, February 11, 2011.

Curtiz, Michael. Director, *Casablanca*, Warner Bros., 1942.

Denning, S. *A Leader's Guide to Storytelling: Mastering the Art and Discipline of Business Narrative*. San Francisco, CA: Jossey-Bass, 2005.

Dickman, R., and R. Maxwell. *The Elements of Persuasion: Use Storytelling to Pitch Better, Sell Faster, and Win More Business*. New York: HarperCollins, 2007.

Forest, H. "The Power of Words: Leadership, Metaphor and Story." Proceedings of 8th Annual International Leadership Association Conference, Leadership at the Crossroads. November 2–5, 2006, Chicago, IL.

Frank, A. *Letting Stories Breathe: A Socio-Narratology*. Chicago: University of Chicago, 2010.

Gaut, B. "Telling Stories: Narration, Emotion, and Insight in Memento." In *Narrative, Emotion, and Insight*. Edited by N. Carroll and J. Gibson. University Park, PA: Pennsylvania State University Press, 2011.

Goldie, P. "Life, Fiction and Narrative." In *Narrative, Emotion and Insight*. Edited by N. Carroll and J. Gibson. University Park, PA: Pennsylvania State University Press, 2011.

Guber, P. *Tell to Win*. New York: Crown Business, 2011

Hewitt, D. *Tell Me a Story: Fifty Years and 60 Minutes in Television*. New York: Public Affairs, 2002.

Hogan, P. *Affective Narratology: The Emotional Structure of Stories.* Lincoln, NE: University of Nebraska Press, 2011.

Horsdal, M. *Telling Lives: Exploring Dimensions of Narratives.* New York: Routledge, 2012.

Kouzes, J., and B. Posner. *Encouraging the Heart: A Leader's Guide to Rewarding and Recognizing Others.* San Francisco, CA: Jossey-Bass. 2003.

Morin, E. "New Trends in the Study of Mass Communications." Proceedings of the Unesco Round Table, September 9–13, 1968, Montreal.

Neyfakh, L. "Why We Give to Charity." *Boston Globe,* December 4, 2011.

Ong, W. *Orality and Literacy.* New York: Routledge, 2002.

Pekar, T. "The Benefits of Building a Narrative Organization." *Stanford Social Innovation Review,* April 22, 2011.

Potter, D., and A. Lang. "The Seven Habits of Highly Effective Storytellers." *RTNDA Communicator Magazine,* October 1999.

Silver, K. "True Story." *Spirit Magazine,* October, 2011: 79–86.

Simmons, A. *The Story Factor: Secrets of Influence from the Art of Storytelling.* New York: Basic Books, 2006.

Stefanovich, A. "Facts vs. Storytelling." www.playstudio.com, 2011.

Waldman, P. *Being Right Is Not Enough.* Hoboken, NJ: John Wiley and Sons, 2006.

Chapter 2: Messaging

Ansolabehere, S., and S. Iyengar. *Going Negative.* New York: The Free Press, 1995.

Carlson, T. *The How of Wow: A Guide to Giving a Speech that will Positively Blow 'em away.* New York: Amacom, 2005.

Berger, C., and M. Roloff. *Social Cognition and Communication:* Beverly Hills, CA: Sage Publications, 1982.

Boyer, M. "News Interview Techniques." www.martyboyer.com, 2011.

Cupach, W., and B. Spitzberg. *Interpersonal Communication Competence.* Beverly Hills, CA: Sage Publications, 1984.

Denton, R., and D. Hahn. *Presidential Communication: Description and Analysis.* New York: Praeger, 1986.

Faucheux, R. *Running for Office: The Strategies, Techniques, and Messages Modern Candidates Need to Win Elections.* Lanham, MD, 2002.

Gallo, C. "How to Pitch Anything in 15 Seconds." www.forbes.com, July 17, 2012.

Heath, C., and D. Heath. *Made to Stick: Why Some Ideas Survive and Others Die.* New York: Random House, 2008.

Heath, C., and D. Heath. *Switch: How to Change Things When Change Is Hard.* New York: Broadway Books, 2010.

Lang, A., P. Bolis, R. Potter, and K. Kawahara. "The Effects of Production Pacing and Arousing Content on the information Processing of Television Messages." *Journal of Broadcasting and Electronic Media,* Fall 2009.

Lowy, A. *The Power of the 2x2 Matrix.* San Francisco, CA: Jossey-Bass. 2004.

McQuail, D. *Communication.* New York: Longman Press, 1984.

Moffitt, M. *Campaign Strategies and Message Design: A Practitioner's Guide from Start to Finish.* Westport, CT: Praeger Publishers, 1999.

Chapter 3: Nonverbal Communication

Birdwhistell, R. *Kinesics and Context: Essays on Body Motion Communication.* Philadelphia, PA: The University of Pennsylvania Press, 1970.

Bosmajian, H. *The Rhetoric of Nonverbal Communication.* Glenview, IL: Scott Foresman and Company, 1996.

Dichter, E. "Testing Nonverbal Communications." *Nonverbal Communication in Advertising.* Edited by S. Hecker. Washington, D.C.: Lexington Books, 1988.

Edell, J. "Nonverbal Effects in Ads: A Review and Synthesis." *Nonverbal Communication in Advertising.* Edited by S. Hecker. Washington, D.C.: Lexington Books, 1988.

Goleman, D. *Emotional Intelligence: Why it Can Matter More Than IQ.* New York: Bantam Books, 1994.

Goman, C. *The Nonverbal Advantage: Secrets and Science of Body Language at Work.* San Francisco, CA: Berrett-Koehler Publishers, 2008.

Goman, C. *The Silent Language of Leaders: How Body Language Can Help—Or Hurt—How You Lead.* San Francisco, CA: Jossey-Bass, 2011.

Harrison, R. *Beyond Words: An Introduction to Nonverbal Communication.* Englewood Cliffs, NJ: Prentice-Hall, 1984.

Kelly, S. D., P. Creigh, and J. Bartolotti. "Integrating speech and iconic gestures in a Stroop-like task: Evidence for automatic processing." *Journal of Cognitive Neuroscience* 22 (2010): 683–694.

Mortensen, C. D., *Communication: The Study of Human Interaction*. New York: Kingsport Press, 1972.

Powell, M. *"In 9/11 Chaos, Giuliani Forged a Lasting Image."* New York Times, September 21, 2007.

Segal, J. *The Language of Emotional Intelligence*. New York: McGraw-Hill, 2008.

Shanteau, J. "Consumer Impression Formation: The Integration of Visual and Verbal Information." *Nonverbal Communication in Advertising*. Edited by S. Hecker. Washington, D.C.: Lexington Books, 1988.

Vancil, D., and S. Pendell. "The Myth of Viewer-Listener Disagreement in the First Kennedy-Nixon Debate." *Central States Speech Journal* Spring 1987: 16–27.

Vargas, M. *Louder than Words: An Introduction to Nonverbal Communication*. Ames, IA: Iowa State Press, 1986.

Chapter 4: Branding

Du Plessis, E. *The Advertised Mind*. Sterling, VA: Kogan Page, 1998.

Englis, B. "Consumer Emotional Reactions to Television Advertising and Their Effects on Message Recall." *Emotion in Advertising: Theoretical and Practical Explorations*. Edited by S. Agres, J. Edell, and T. Dubitsky. New York: Quorum, 1990.

Freiberg, K., and J. Freiberg. *Nuts!: Southwest Airlines' Crazy Recipe for Business and Personal Success*. New York: Broadway Books, 1997.

Gobe, M. *Emotional Branding: The New Paradigm for Connecting Brands to People*. New York: Allworth Press, 2009.

Goldman, R., and S. Papson. *Nike Culture: The Sign of the Swoosh*. Thousand Oaks, CA: Sage Publications, 2000.

Gross, D. *Forbes Greatest Business Stories of All Time*. New York: John Wiley and Sons, 1996.

Healey, M. *What Is Branding?* Mies, Switzerland: Rotovision Books, 2008.

Kahney, L. "Apple: It's all about the Brand." www.wired.com, Decemeber 4, 2002.

Kelly, F., and B. Silverstein. *The Breakaway Brand: How Great Brands Stand Out*. New York: McGraw-Hill, 2005.

Koehn, N. "The Starbucks Debate." *The Economist,* June 13, 2011.

Landa, R. *Designing Brand Experiences.* Clifton Park, NY: Thomson Delmar Learning, 2006.

Marconi, J. *Public Relations: The Complete Guide.* Clifton Park, NY: Thomson, 2004.

Millman, D. *Brand Thinking and Other Noble Pursuits.* New York: Allworth Press, 2009.

Napoletano, E. "What Every Entrepreneur Can Learn from Hair Club for Men." www.entrepreneur.com,October 30, 2011.

Raphael, T. *The President Electric: Ronald Reagan and the Politics of Performance.* Ann Arbor, MI: University of Michigan Press, 2009.

Rivkin, S., and F. Sutherland. *The Making of a Name: The Inside Story of the Brands We Buy.* New York: Oxford University Press, 2004.

Satran, R. "Starbucks Is the Best Loved Food Brand on Social Media." www.nbcnews.com, September 5, 2012.

Solis, B. *Engage!* Hoboken, NJ: John Wiley and Sons, 2011.

Teresko, J. "The Toyota Branding System?" *Industry Week,* January 19, 2007.

Ware, L. *Selling It: The Incredible Shrinking Package and Other Marvels of Modern Marketing.* New York: W. W. Norton and Company, 2002.

Chapter 5: Images

Adkins Covert, T. *Manipulating Images: World War II Mobilization of Women through Magazine Advertising.* New York: Rowman and Middlefield, 2012.

Agres, S. "Emotion in Advertising: An Agency Point of View." In *Emotion in Advertising: Theoretical and Practical Explorations.* Edited by S. Agres, J. Edell, and T. Dubitsky. New York: Quorum, 1990.

Barron-Simpson, M. "CDC Coffee Break: Communicating About Data." Internal Presentation Given to Centers for Disease Control, July 12, 2011.

Du Plessis, E. *The Advertised Mind.* Sterling, VA: Kogan Page, 1998.

Greyser, S. A. *Cases in Advertising and Communications Management.* 3rd ed. Englewood Cliffs, NJ: Prentice Hall, 1992.

Hamlin, S. *How to Talk So People Listen.* New York: HarperCollins, 1988.

Kanner, B. *The Super Bowl of Advertising: How Commercials Won the Game.* New York: Bloomberg Press, 2003.

Lester, P. "Syntactic Theory of Visual Communication." http://commfaculty.fullerton.edu/lester/writings/viscomtheory.html. 2006.

Mayer, R., and R. Moreno. "Instructional Technology." *Handbook of Applied Cognition*. Edited by F. Durso. Hoboken, NJ: John Wiley and Sons, 2011.

Monson, M. "Communicating Effectively: Word Pictures." www.monsoncommunications.com. 2010.

Paivio, A. *Mental Representations: A Dual Coding Approach*. New York: Oxford University Press, 1990.

Rupp, Leila J. *Mobilizing Women for War: German and American Propaganda, 1939–1945*. Princeton, NJ: Princeton University Press, 1978.

Saks, F. "Effects on Blood Pressure of Reduced Dietary Sodium and the Dietary Approaches to Stop Hypertension." *New England Journal of Medicine*, January 4, 2011.

Ware, L. *Selling It: The Incredible Shrinking Package and Other Marvels of Modern Marketing*. New York: W. W. Norton and Company, 2002.

Weiss, H., and J. McGrath. *Technically Speaking: Oral Communication for Engineers, Scientists, and Technical Personnel*. New York: McGraw-Hill, 1963.

Winston, B. *Messages: Free Expression, Media, and the West from Gutenberg to Google*. New York: Routledge, 2005.

Chapter 6: Framing

Baumgartner, F., and S. Linn. "The Decline of the Death Penalty: How Media Framing Changed Capital Punishment in America." *Winning with Words: The Origins and Impact of Political Framing*. Edited by P. Sellers and B. Schaffner. New York: Routledge, 2010.

Brewer, P., and K. Gross. "Studying the Effects of Framing on Public Opinion about Policy Issues." *Doing News Framing Analysis*. Edited by P. D'Angelo and J. Kuypers. New York: Routledge, 2010.

Coleman, R. "Framing the Pictures in our Heads." In D'Angelo P. and Kuypers, J. (ed.) *Doing News Framing Analysis*. New York: Routledge, 2010.

Iyengar, S. "Framing Research: The Next Steps." In *Winning with Words: The Origins and Impact of Political Framing*. Edited by P. Sellers and B. Schaffner. New York: Routledge, 2010.

Nisbet, M. "Knowledge into Action: Framing the Debates over Climate Change and Poverty." *Doing News Framing Analysis.* Edited by P. D'Angelo P. and J. Kuypers. New York: Routledge, 2010.

Feldman, J. *Framing the Debate.* New York: Ig, 2007.

Fairhurst, G. *The Power of Framing.* San Francisco, CA: Jossey-Bass, 2010.

Fairhurst, G., and R. Sarr. *The Art of Framing.* San Francisco, CA: Jossey-Bass, 1996.

Lakoff, G. *Don't Think of an Elephant!* White River Junction, VT: Chelsea Green Publishing, 2005.

Malhotra, N., and M. Yotam. "Marketing Obama's Stimulus Package: Insights from Social Science Experiments on Public Opinion." Research paper. Stanford Graduate School of Business, 2008.

Nelson, T., and D. Wittmer. "Framing and Value Recruitment in the Debate Over Teaching Evolution." *Winning with Words: The Origins and Impact of Political Framing.* Edited by P. Sellers and B. Schaffner. New York: Routledge, 2010.

Schaffner, B., and M. Atkinson. "Taxing Death or Estates? When Frames Influence Citizens' Issue Beliefs." *Winning with Words: The Origins and Impact of Political Framing.* Edited by P. Sellers and B. Schaffner. New York: Routledge, 2010.

Sellers, P., and B. Schaffner. *Winning with Words: The Origins and Impact of Political Framing.* New York: Routledge, 2010.

Chapter 7: Social Media

Blackshaw, P. *Satisfied Customers Tell Three Friends, Angry Customers Tell 3,000.* New York: Doubleday, 2008.

Breakenridge, D. *PR 2.0: New Media, New Tools, New Audiences.* Upper Saddle River, NJ: FT Press, 2008.

Byers, D. "Blink: The 21-minute News Cycle." *www.politico.com,* August 27, 2012.

Finnell, J. "Gresham's Law in the 21st Century." *Electronic Journal of Academic and Special Librarianship* 10, no. 1 (Spring 2009).

Goldstein, N., and S. Martin. *"Yes!: 50 Scientifically Proven Ways to Be Persuasive."* New York: Free Press, 2008.

Goodman, J., and J. Preston. "How the KONY Video Went Viral." *New York Times,* March 12, 2012.

Holiday, R. *Trust Me, I'm Lying: Confessions of a Media Manipulator.* New York: Penguin Books, 2012.

Hovland, C., and I. Janis. *Communication and Persuasion.* Westport, CT: Greenwood Press, 1953.

Katz, E. "The Two-Step Flow of Communication: An Up-to-Date Report on an Hypothesis." University of Pennsylvania, http://repository. upenn.edu/cgi/viewcontent.cgi?article=1279&context=asc_papers. 1957.

Keller, E., and B. Fay. *The Face-to-Face Book: Why Real Relationships Rule in a Digital Marketplace.* New York: Free Press, 2012.

Penenberg, A. *Viral Loop: From Facebook to Twitter: How Today's Smartest Businesses Grow Themselves.* New York: Hyperion, 2009.

Rainey, J. "Group Behind KONY Wins New Respect." *Los Angeles Times,* June 30, 2012.

Sernovitz, A. *Word of Mouth Marketing: How Smart Companies Get People Talking.* Chicago, IL: Kaplan, 2006.

Sarkar, C. "Interview with Hal Varian: The Economics of Information." www.christiansarkar.com, October 31, 2009.

Wasserman, T. "KONY 2012 Tops 100 Million Views: Becomes the most Viral Video in History." www.mashable.com, March 12, 2012.

Chapter 8: Theory

Aikins, A. "Nonverbal Communication in Everyday Multicultural Life." *The Social Psychology of Communication.* Edited by D. Hook and B. Franks. New York: Palgrave MacMillan, 2011.

Andersen, P., and L. Guerrero. "Principles of Communication and Emotion in Social Interaction." *Handbook of Communication and Emotion.* San Diego, CA: Academic Press, 1998.

Andrzejewski, S., and J. Hall. "Who Draws Accurate First Impressions?" *First Impressions.* Edited by M. Ambay and J. Skowronski. New York: Guilford Press, 2008.

Lin, N. *The Study of Human Communication.* New York: The Bobbs-Merrill Company, 1974.

Mehrabian, A. *Nonverbal Communication.* Chicago, IL: Aldine-Atherton, 1972.

Ong, W. *Orality and Literacy.* New York: Routledge, 2002.

Page, T., E. Thorson, and M. Heide. "The Memory Impact of Commercials Varying in Emotional Appeal and Product Development." *Emo-*

tion in Advertising: Theoretical and Practical Explorations. Edited by S. Agres, J. Edell, and T. Dubitsky. New York: Quorum, 1990.

Planalp, S. "Communicating Emotion in Everyday Life: Cues, Channels and Processes." Handbook of Communication and Emotion. Edited by P. Andersen and L. Guerro. San Diego, CA: Academic Press, 1998.

Poe, M. A History of Communications: Media and Society from the Evolution of Speech to the Internet. New York: Cambridge University Press, 2011.

Schaller, M. "Evolutionary Bases of First Impressions." First Impressions. Edited by M. Ambay and J. Skowronski. New York: Guilford Press, 2008.

INDEX

Zach Friend is a policy, public affairs, and communications expert who has worked for Barack Obama and John Kerry's presidential campaigns, the White House Council of Economic Advisers, the U.S. Senate and U.S. House of Representatives and the Democratic National Committee. With Obama for America '08, he was a press secretary and spokesman in the battleground state of Pennsylvania. He's been quoted by MSNBC, Fox News, CNN, ABC, CBS, NPR, the *LA Times,* the *Boston Globe,* and Politico and is a blogger for the *Huffington Post* and *Business Insider.*